We Carry
Our Homes
With Us

We Carry
Our Homes
With Us

A Cuban American Memoir

MARISELLA VEIGA

MINNESOTA
HISTORICAL
SOCIETY PRESS

"Rolling" originally published in the *Mid-American Review* 12.1
(Bowling Green, OH, 1991).

www.mnhspress.org

All photos, unless noted, courtesy of the author and her family.

The Minnesota Historical Society Press is a member of the Association
of American University Presses.

Manufactured in the United States of America

10 9 8 7 6 5 4 3 2 1

♾ The paper used in this publication meets the minimum
requirements of the American National Standard for Information
Sciences—Permanence for Printed Library Materials,
ANSI Z39.48–1984.

International Standard Book Number

ISBN: 978-1-68134-006-7 (paper)

ISBN: 978-1-68134-007-4 (e-book)

Library of Congress Cataloging-in-Publication Data
available upon request.

This and other Minnesota Historical Society Press books
are available from popular e-book vendors

We Carry Our Homes With Us is set in the Dante typeface family.

Book design and typesetting by
BNTypographics West Ltd., Victoria, B.C. Canada

Printed by Versa Press, East Peoria, Illinois

For my beloved father

and

in memory of

MARK E. WEKANDER (1951–2014)

son of the Midwest, writer, friend

⌈ A C K N O W L E D G M E N T S ⌉

There are no words in English or Spanish to convey the gratitude I have for my editor, Pamela McClanahan. She identified this story as important, then dedicated time and talent to its telling. Her editorial direction was insightful, intelligent, and compassionate. My deepest thanks go to her.

I appreciate the contributions of Minnesota Historical Society Press staff and its freelance collaborators.

Many thanks to Robert Hedin and the staff at the Anderson Center for Interdisciplinary Studies in Red Wing, Minnesota. Their hospitality and care during a month-long residency enabled me to write an early draft.

Research assistance given by the reference librarians at the Flagler College Library is much appreciated.

Besides sharing stories, family members contributed in myriad ways. I am grateful for the prayers and encouragement of the Veiga, Echevarria, and González families as well as those of the Rettigs.

Countless people expressed their good wishes during the writing of this book. I appreciate their interest and the generosity of their spirits. Special thanks to Keti Beguiristain, Tina Bucuvalas, Sudye Cauthen, Carol and Joe Dietrick, Jacob Jones, Una Kruse, Paula Morton, Ruben Nazario, Mimi Pink, and P. C. Zick.

Heartfelt thanks to my husband, Dick Rettig, who is a steadfast companion. Thanks, Sweetie, for coming along on the ride.

Rolling

I've been rolling all along
Simply rolling.
See how smooth my shoulders are.

The stones know my body
And I know theirs.
They are hard, like mahogany.

I have smelled their minerals.
The stones, at times,
Were small fish swimming about.

I wanted to catch and set
Them out to dry
But the smart things rolled away.

Once, I thought I could not rise
Away from them
And keep moving on the ground.

I piled them into a ring
And like a fire
I leapt—but returned, centered.

No one steps over the ring.
I press my face
Into the warm stones and sigh.

Marisella Veiga

We Carry
Our Homes
With Us

[CHAPTER I]

M y father, Miguel Veiga, watched the rural landscape roll by from the window of a station wagon, disturbed by what he saw. The architecture of midwestern farming was new to him—big red barns, silver silos, tightly planted cornfields rolling for acres toward the sky. And now, thanks to his American hosts, the Lauer farm in Mendota Heights, Minnesota, was where his next home, though temporary, would be. In a week's time my mother and siblings and I would join him.

A few short years before, he and my mother had chosen the fishing village of Cojímar for their home. In fifteen minutes, they could be in cosmopolitan Havana. My father loved the city, especially for its architectural elegance.

That was before. This was now.

Cubans are familiar with sugarcane fields, banana plantations, and citrus groves. In addition to those, my father knew coastal landmarks, especially docks, fishing fleets, and warehouses storing natural sponges. His father had worked in that industry on both the southern and northern coasts of Cuba.

At thirty-nine, he and my mother, Maria González de Veiga, thirty-six, had decided to move from Miami, their initial place of exile, to the Upper Midwest. The move to Minnesota was miles from the subtropics and even farther from a past that remained hidden in their minds and hearts. The enormous loss of homeland had left them speechless, unable to speak about what they'd left behind. Thinking, talking, or crying about it was a luxury.

The need for survival demanded they focus on the present. By doing so, they would begin to lay a foundation to ensure a good future for themselves and, more importantly, for their children.

I am one of those children, their oldest daughter. I have an older and a younger brother and younger sister. My sister was conceived in Miami and born in St. Paul, a few months after we resettled there.

The move north was risky—our exile community was largely in Miami. However, considering Miami's economic conditions in the early 1960s and the large numbers of Cubans fleeing the island, resettlement away from South Florida (in our case to Minnesota) was a better choice in many ways. In a 1963 report on the Cuban Refugee Program, John F. Thomas writes, "The difficulties which refugees face in Miami and the importance of the resettlement program are highlighted by the fact that about 58 percent of the refugees in Miami require financial assistance compared with less than 5 percent of those resettled [elsewhere]." Economic independence was key.

"Even the grass is different here," my father thought as Al Lauer drove to a church reception. My father didn't share the observation with his hosts.

He was remembering Cojímar, the fishing village where he and my mother had bought property on a hilltop. His cousin Raul had designed the modern house that overlooked the bay. The constant breezes onto Cuba's north coast were delicious. The house benefited from them. When my parents bought the property, they believed there was no better place in the world to live. They planned to be buried there.

That place was gone.

More specifically, they had left it. They opted for freedoms for themselves and for their children, freedoms that would be denied under the new regime.

Forty-five minutes after our initial flight out of the country, we landed in Miami. In many ways, though work was scarce, Miami was comfortable as far as identifying culturally and politically. Its climate was similar to Cuba's. The beaches were good. Thousands like us flew into town every month. The Spanish language returned to Florida. Most of the familiar tropical fruits and root vegetables were available. Native Miamians and retired Northerners in South Florida began adjusting to our arrival. If they couldn't, they listed their homes and moved to Broward County or even farther north.

When we relocated to Minnesota we would be seen as aliens, outsiders—our first experience with this in exile.

After five years in Minnesota, my father had become comfortable with wool outerwear. He owned a black coat, a forest-green short-brimmed hat, a plaid scarf, and deerskin gloves with a double wool lining. Every weekday for work he wore a suit and tie, though sometimes he picked a clip bow tie. He looked the part of a company comptroller. The weekday commute from Roseville to downtown St. Paul took fifteen minutes, about the same time it took to commute from Cojímar to Havana. By that time, he'd learned that some mornings it took longer than that to shovel the driveway.

One particular morning, he remembers, it wasn't so cold in the garage. He started the car to warm the engine and went back to lift the garage door. He faced a wall of snow. He stood before it, so he said, and thought, "What am I, a Cuban, doing here? Nothing in my life has prepared me for this."

In the Caribbean, people don't receive instruction on survival skills for cold climates. There is no need for it. The tropics have their lessons: hurricane preparedness, shark bite avoidance, malaria and dengue fever treatments. Moreover, during my parents' last years in Cuba they became quick studies in dealing with annoying, then menacing revolutionaries.

He turned for the snow shovel and imagined a future evolving for his family in a place farther south.

Like many of the other Cubans who resettled in Minnesota, my parents weren't prepared for drastic climate and cultural changes or extended exile. They adjusted to some ways and raised their eyebrows at others. They watched their children adopt these American ways—some questionable. While they accepted that changes were inevitable, I am sure they found some of our new ways painful, especially regarding family relationships.

For one thing, my siblings and I moved across the United States for better educational and job opportunities, especially as young adults. Such dispersal of family members is not as common in Cuba. While a family member might move to other provinces, the country is small enough to facilitate regular contact. The size of the United States makes frequent visits difficult to manage. Unfortunately, this dispersal, along with the money and time needed to overcome it, has resulted in less familiarity with my nieces and nephews.

Furthermore, my brothers and I married outside of our original Roman Catholic faith, uncommon for our family back in Cuba. Luis Gustavo, my older brother, is now Pastor Lou, an ordained Presbyterian minister with a Houston-based church. His wife and children are Presbyterian. My younger brother, Juan Carlos, now John, attends a nondenominational mega-church in

McLean, Virginia, with his wife and children; his wife is a former Presbyterian. Meanwhile, I attend a Catholic Mass on Sunday while my husband attends a Presbyterian service. I sometimes join him there.

People learn to live in exile—no matter where one sets up housekeeping—by experiencing it. Exile is a state of being that continues for most Cubans who live outside their country if they have left for political, not economic, reasons. It ends when Cuba embraces democracy. If and when this transpires, the number of exiles who will return to the island remains to be seen.

With two exceptions, my family members who came to the United States were born in Cuba and raised in households with its customs. Therefore, it is natural for us to self-identify as Cubans who are U.S. citizens.

However, other differences exist.

Over the more than fifty years our family has lived in the United States, family members have assimilated at different rates. Each person has adopted norms that ease the way in the larger culture. Still the fact remains: we have dual identities. That is one way of beginning to describe what it means to be a Cuban raised in the United States, part of what it is to be bicultural.

My older brother, Luis Gustavo, was born in 1955. I was born in 1957. Our younger brother Juan Carlos was born in 1959. That year, Fidel Castro took control of the government from a former Cuban president who'd returned to the island from Daytona Beach, Florida, to become a dictator: Fulgencio Batista.

Since my earliest memories are from Cuba, my natural home, they are precious to me and I've kept them alive by reviewing them. Most are set on the grounds of our family's house in Cojímar. To date, it is the only brand-new house I've lived in.

Ernest Hemingway kept his boat in Cojímar. Santiago, the protagonist in *The Old Man and the Sea,* is based on a Cuban fisherman who lived near the bay; from a humble home there, he set out in a skiff to make a living from the sea, as the fishermen there still do.

I lived in Cojímar from the time I came home from the Havana clinic until my mother and two brothers and I boarded a flight to Miami on December 30, 1960.

I have eight-by-ten black-and-white photographs of my first home. Although it is high on a hill, the midcentury modern house sits on stilts, like many of the houses in the Florida Keys. It weathers flooding due to hurricane rains and winds. It withstands high winds since it is made of poured, reinforced concrete with a monolithic roof of the same material. My father's first cousin, Raul Arcia, designed it to last.

Three bedrooms, a bathroom, dining room, kitchen, and living room are upstairs. A double garage is on the ground level. Next to it is a bedroom with a full bathroom reserved for guests or a live-in helper. In those days, my parents employed a housekeeper who often stayed the night rather than take a bus back to her town only to return to work by bus the following morning.

Six properties sat at the top of the hill. Jaime Rabel and his wife and son lived to the west of our house. He was a hardware salesman who traveled the island. The neighbor to the east has attracted more interest. Fidel Castro lived next door and, as of this writing, still does so occasionally. His is a large house with about two acres of land, a property that once belonged to Tinito Cruz-Fernández, a senator, and his wife. They were killed in an accident while vacationing in Spain.

A few weeks after the revolutionaries took control of the government, a guardhouse and a chain were installed at the head of our short street. Guards were posted. They searched vehicles leaving and entering the street. My father's car was not exempt. They searched his 1956 Chevrolet Bel Air when he left for work in the morning and when he returned in the afternoon.

One day, my father remembered, as he waited for the guards to finish a routine search, he noticed Jaime Rabel's car stopped behind his. Behind Rabel's car was another vehicle with a well-known passenger: Che Guevara. My father drove home after being cleared. Che's car stopped in front of Rabel's house. Che signaled for my father to join them.

"What I've just seen, that shouldn't be," said Che. "This wasn't the purpose of the revolution."

My father explained such searches were common practice.

"I'm going to give orders so this doesn't happen," Che said.

"Look, *Commandante,* I appreciate your concern, but it's not going to work. Fidel has given orders for everyone to be searched, and that's how it's going to be," my father said.

"I'm going to change it. This shouldn't be happening."

"Will you give me your phone number so I can call you right after we're searched again?" my father asked.

The next day, Rabel and my father joked about Che's belief that he would alter Fidel's order. The search order wasn't revoked.

The backyard of our house faced north and had a gentle slope. Luis Gustavo and I often played there on our swing set. A dirt road was at the northern edge. That path was forbidden. One day, I chased Luis Gustavo. Other children had caught his attention on that dirt road. He was about five years old and had more freedom. After a hard run, I stopped at the end of our yard where the grass met the dirt road. I looked to my left. A group of boys was hanging on a jeep or a cart. They were dressed in green military clothing. Luis ran to play with them. I returned to the yard where my grandmother Manuela waited, annoyed with my disobedience and maybe even with herself for the lapse in supervision.

The other memory is a scene, not a full story: I'm playing in a fountain with a limestone rock in the center that was in the cool patio area under the stilts of the house. My brother is nearby. I like to think we have an appreciation for one another born during those years, the cherished ones when we were play-mates who lived in our own country and spoke only Spanish. Our younger brother Juan Carlos didn't walk yet, was still a baby.

The two memories don't reveal much. I have scanned them for clues to who I was back then, for hints of the person I was supposed to become. Once, I believed I would be satisfied if I could get in touch with the essence of that monolingual child with one set of customs. I would be complete, whole. In other words, I would be the person I was intended to be when I was born, a Cuban at home, not an outsider to people in two countries.

Life would be easier! I would cease evaluating and reconciling two halves, two cultures, two languages. My status as a child of two nations and not completely of either would evaporate.

Yet these are the adult musings of a person who moved from innocence to experience by age three. I long for a little more time in the former state. It would have been nice, I think. The nostalgia is born from a state of innocence cut short.

In December 1960, as Luis and I ran through the backyards and beaches during our last days on the island, the Cuban Refu-gee Emergency Center, called *El Refugio* by the newcomers, was set up in Miami inside the Freedom Tower on Biscayne Boule-vard. The $1 million funds for the center came from President Eisenhower's contingency fund under the Mutual Security Act of 1954. With this help from the U.S. government and from friends who opened their crowded home to give us shelter, we had a soft landing in Miami, our first, temporary U.S. home.

Two years before arriving in Minnesota, my father lived the saddest day of his life: December 30, 1960. That day he watched his wife, Maria, thirty-four, and my brothers and me board a KLM Royal Dutch Airlines airplane at the José Martí International Airport in Havana. Juan Carlos remembers standing on the tarmac, holding our mother's hand and crying. This is his first childhood memory. He was fifteen months old.

That was my last day in Cuba for fifty years. That same day, my brothers and I took our first steps in the United States. We were on the wide and often lonely road to a bicultural life.

The Cuban influx was different from other migrations to the United States. For one, we were not previously screened by the U.S. government in our country of origin. Furthermore, we lacked sponsors to vouch for us. Like most Cubans who were leaving at this time, we simply boarded an airplane with our one suitcase apiece—we said we were going to a wedding—and in less than an hour we were in a new city as refugees. Between January 1959 and January 1961, some fifty thousand Cubans had left for the United States. More than thirty-seven thousand arrived in Miami Dade County. Like most of our compatriots, my parents hoped the stay wouldn't be long.

Fairly quickly, a dual identity for Cubans like us was formalized by U.S. law. In his book *Americans at the Gate: The United States and Refugees during the Cold War,* Carl J. Bon Tempo writes, "Most remarkably, the Cuban Status Adjustment Act led politicians, refugee advocates, and Cuban refugees themselves to endorse a bifurcated citizenship in which Cubans might become permanent residents or citizens while still planning to return to the island. Status normalization, in the case of Cuban refugees, condoned divided loyalties. No previous refugee group, or immigrant group for that matter, had been granted such leeway."

From Miami International Airport, we went to Southwest Twelfth Street to stay with Celia and Paco Vasquez and their two daughters, Delsa and Nora. They were my mother's lifelong friends from Punta San Juan, the location of the Punta Alegre Sugar Mill in Camaguey, Cuba. They hosted us for a little more than a week.

In January 1961, my mother, who spoke some English, rented a small one-bedroom house with a den in northwest Miami, on Northwest 54th Street and Seventh Avenue. She lacked a telephone. Thankfully, the American landlord took messages and relayed them. His telephone remained available for vital calls.

Great-aunt Carmen Ballesteros Echevarria and her husband, Great-uncle Epifanio Echevarria, moved with us. Their exile had begun a month earlier. Soon, crowded conditions forced Epifanio to move temporarily to Kankakee, Illinois, with his son and daughter-in-law, Orlando and Carol Echevarria.

The United States broke off diplomatic relations with Cuba on January 3, 1961. The following month, with a valid travel visa, my mother returned to the island to join my father. A Cuban can always return to the island. My siblings and I stayed in Miami with Great-aunt Carmen.

My mother traveled with empty suitcases in order to pack more clothes, a few books, and some photographs. We care for these portable relics. I store two dresses made for me by my maternal grandfather's sister Rosa in Caibarién, Cuba. My mother's Larousse Spanish dictionary is on my bookshelf. There are a few other things. However, and I am most grateful for this, our family's greatest treasures are intangible. Our biggest inheritances are faith in God, strength of family, and commitment to education.

One of the benefits of exile is that I pack and travel lightly. I am not burdened by needing to house quality furniture that has been passed down and is now antique. My dining room chairs aren't mahogany but cherry. I don't care for my parents' wedding china. A cousin keeps it safe in her cabinets in Cuba. I was fifty-three years old before I saw it. I have no desire to own it.

Before leaving the island, my mother stored a few goods with her aunt in Caibarién, including her wedding dress. Long ago, it was cut apart, its fabric meeting other people's need for clothing.

The last day my parents stood in their native land was February 24, 1961. My father had the foresight to buy tickets on the twice-weekly KLM flight, shunning the popular twice-daily Pan American airlines in case the countries severed diplomatic relations. He wasn't taking chances on having to stay. He also bought KLM tickets for his parents, Miguel and Evangelina Veiga, who left for Miami the same year. Although diplomatic relations with the United States no longer existed, Cubans could travel into and out of the island with appropriate visas. By October 1962, civilian flights to the United States were banned in Cuba.

In 2015, the United States reestablished diplomatic relations with Cuba, opening an embassy there. In 2010 and 2011, I traveled to the island, along with thousands of other Cubans and Americans who live in the United States. Then and now, a visa is required.

My father left his Spanish classical guitar on top of his bed in Cojímar. My mother's first cousin Alfredo drove my parents to the airport in a Chevrolet Bel Air, a green-and-white four-door sedan. My father implored my mother not to look back.

"We're going to die in another country. It will take fifty to sixty years for the revolution to run its course," he said.

He had read about Poland, Yugoslavia, Hungary, and Russia.

In their grief, they agreed to focus on the future in order to ensure our family's survival in a new land.

Alfredo would care for the house and car until there was a real possibility of returning. Officially, he was the new owner of both, as the titles had been transferred to him. Alfredo had his own house in Havana, so ours would be a second home. If the political situation changed, we'd return to the house.

When Alfredo arrived from the airport to the house, he put the key in the front door and turned it. Then a few guards stepped toward him.

"You have to leave this place," they said, taking the keys to the house and car. When we last spoke, Alfredo was eighty-one; he described the experience as traumatic.

Eventually, Alfredo became a political prisoner. He was arrested and jailed twice; once for counterrevolutionary activity, another time for having contraband in the form of U.S. dollars and gold coins. In 1979, he went into exile in the United States.

As Alfredo was dealing with the guards at the house on the hill, my mother boarded the KLM flight without suitcases, which had to be searched. My father brought the suitcases. He was detained for two hours and the flight waited. The guards suspected my father of carrying Fernández family money out of the country. At the time, my father was the general manager for his uncle's business, a lumber company called José Fernández e Hijos.

Besides clothes and photographs, my parents packed accounting textbooks and other reference books. My father used the English-language accounting textbooks at the University of Havana. They remain on the bookshelves in his Miami house.

One by one, the guards paged through the books to see if any money was hidden among the pages. Finally, my father appealed to the guards' reasoning. If he were taking money out of the country, wouldn't it be foolish to hide it in the suitcases? They agreed. He boarded the airplane without being strip-searched.

My father carried a total of fourteen U.S. cents in his pocket, a dime and four brown pennies.

When my parents arrived in Miami, they went to the little rented house on Northwest 54th Street. For three months, they kept us sheltered with a $100 monthly stipend from the U.S. government. Surplus food was distributed to refugees. They welcomed the protein—powdered milk and powdered eggs, peanut butter, and canned meat.

From there, my parents rented a larger house with two bedrooms. It was on Northwest 79th Street and Sixth Avenue. My great-aunt and uncle moved with us.

Meanwhile, the U.S. government had a view about our presence—temporary. In *Havana, U.S.A.: Cuban Exiles and Cuban Americans in South Florida,* Maria Cristina Garcia explains how the Eisenhower administration viewed the Cuban influx. She writes,

> This was the first time the United States had served as the country of first asylum for a group of refugees, he [Eisenhower] argued, and the Cubans' plight deserved a generous response. In reality, however, the administration simply regarded the Cubans as temporary visitors. In March 1960, on the advice of Vice President Richard M. Nixon, Eisenhower approved a CIA plan to train a military invasion force that would 'resolve the Cuban crisis' once and for all. Thus, elaborate relief programs and strict quotas were unnecessary. The Cubans were not to be assimilated but rather assisted until they could resume their normal lives back in Cuba.

That plan was inherited by the new administration of John F. Kennedy in 1962; however, some changes ensued. When the Bay of Pigs invasion failed on April 17, 1961, my parents had to admit that returning to Cuba was impossible, as my father had predicted. To survive, they repressed or ignored their sadness over the loss. Survival trumped all.

Meanwhile, every month, Orlando and Carol Echevarria mailed his parents a check for $100. Orlando's mother, my great-aunt Carmen, was a proud Spaniard. She had refused the $100 monthly government stipend because, as she said, "My son is a doctor." Indeed, Orlando was a medical doctor, a graduate of the medical school at the Universidad Complutense de Madrid in Spain. However, he was unlicensed in the United States and completing his residency at a psychiatric hospital in Ohio; he and Carol were awaiting the birth of their first child, Orlando Jr.

In our little house in Miami, I burned the inside of my left arm on an iron. Juan Carlos cut his finger on a razor blade while reaching for something on a dresser. The noise of the Goodyear blimp stimulated the neighborhood dogs to incessant barking. Juan Carlos cried with the racket they made.

In that same house, despite our great-aunt's warnings, Luis Gustavo continued to play with a ball inside. Once, he threw it up to the living room ceiling, where it hit the square glass lighting fixture. I watched it unwind from its screw and crash on his head.

One of my most vivid memories of our early days in Miami involves a trip to a department store, probably a Woolworth's, with my mother and great-aunt. We passed a toy section where I was drawn to a black plastic doll. I wanted it so badly I threw a tantrum. My mother pulled me along, saying no. There was no money for a doll.

Since it is one of my few early memories, I have replayed it countless times to make sense of the incident. Clearly, I wanted a new doll. Over the years, my adult desire to understand a memory from a crucial time period resulted in many questions. I layered the incident with conjecture. Did I want the black doll because the plastic pink ones with yellow hair were so ugly? Was I drawn to the black doll because of my own complexion—olive skin, brown eyes and hair? Did I just want a new doll? Was I a spoiled child?

In 2010, on my first trip to Cuba after fifty years, those questions were answered. At the José Martí International Airport, I waited for the chartered flight back to the United States. I had a few Cuban dollars left so I was browsing the merchandise on tables outside of the cigar and alcohol store. There, I spotted a book by the beloved patriot and writer José Martí. *The Black Doll* is a Cuban classic. Without a doubt, the story of the girl and her love for her black doll was one that had been read to me as a child. I paid very little for a copy of the book. Fifty years of guesswork was resolved by an accidental discovery.

Luis Gustavo's first experience with cultural misunderstandings occurred in this same Miami house. As the oldest child, he was a scout venturing into the English-speaking world of Little River Elementary School. He started first grade, where he learned how George Washington confessed to chopping down a family cherry tree. Luis was impressed.

One day, Luis played a game in the backyard, alone. He ran full tilt toward a metal T-pole that held clotheslines. He'd grab the pole with one hand and spin around it until he tumbled to the ground. It was great fun, he remembers, until he brought the pole down. The clotheslines were loaded with clean laundry.

He feared our mother's discipline but took a chance on being forgiven, since George Washington had received a reprieve. Luis went inside the house to confess. Our mother ran to the window and wailed. Clean laundry on a sandy yard! The work it took to wash, wring, and hang it!

Cubans didn't care about Washington as much as their laundry, he concluded.

From this same house we walked under I-95 to visit our paternal grandparents, Miguel and Evangelina Veiga, who lived nearby in a rented house. They stayed in Miami when we resettled to Minnesota.

Years ago, the house on Northwest 79th Street and a few others next to it were demolished. A hotel replaced them. It has changed hands several times but remains in business, though I wouldn't rent a room there today.

I pass it when I drive south to the end of I-95 when I visit my parents in southwest Miami. I look to the right when the signs announce Northwest 79th Street. I like to note the place where my U.S. life began.

"That's where we lived when we came from Cuba," I think. "When we came from Cuba."

If there are passengers, I point to the hotel and say the words aloud.

From this house, my parents went to work. My mother, a licensed optometrist and pharmacist in Cuba, found part-time work at Woolworth's. I can see her behind the counter, flipping hamburgers, happy to see her aunt and children who'd come to visit.

My father found work at the Deauville Hotel on Miami Beach as a night auditor. On May 1, when the tourist season ended, the proprietors announced they were going north to the mountains in the Carolinas where they operated another hotel. They invited my father to join them.

However, my father didn't want to relocate us for the summer. Instead, he took a temporary job with a friend who had opened a warehouse. He moved boxes, sorted beans—in short, did whatever was required to keep a regular paycheck.

Jobs were scarce in Miami as a result of the flood of refugees, about eighteen hundred a week. Employers with jobs for unskilled labor found many applicants to be English-speaking, professional Cubans eager to work. The competition for these jobs was keen.

My parents had registered at the Cuban Refugee Center, though doing so was not required. After the failure of the Bay of Pigs invasion my parents evaluated Miami's economic situation and tallied the number of refugees. They returned to the center, registering for resettlement with Catholic Relief Services.

At the time President John F. Kennedy gave the Cuban Refugee Program with the Department of Health, Education, and Welfare funds to help refugees. Monies were provided for assisting volunteer relief agencies, obtaining help from private and public sectors to find jobs, giving funds for resettlement, and giving financial help to cover basic human needs, including health services.

The U.S. federal government also pumped money into Miami public schools, which were racially segregated at the time. Training and educational opportunities were created. Unaccompanied children received financial aid, and surplus food distribution was enhanced.

Four national agencies joined efforts with the federal government to help with the resettlement process: Catholic Relief Services of the National Catholic Welfare Conference, Church World Service of the National Conference of Churches, a Protestant organization, United Hebrew Immigrant Aid Society, and the nonsectarian International Rescue Committee. On a statewide level, civic organizations worked with religious ones.

During the summer of 1962, the U.S. Governors' Conference met in Hershey, Pennsylvania. In the proceedings from that meeting, the governors acknowledged Florida's welcoming of about eighteen hundred Cubans each week. They thanked Florida for its hospitality and resolved to urge the people of all states to help in resettlement efforts.

Through Catholic Relief Services, my father learned there were opportunities for employment in the Midwest, specifically Cincinnati, Ohio, Grand Rapids, Michigan, and St. Paul, Minnesota. Three viable jobs opened in Minnesota. Meanwhile, the Lauers, a Roman Catholic family, had read the dossier about our family that Catholic Relief Services provided their church. They decided to sponsor us. Resettlement, in the end, was by invitation only. We were blessed.

As my father made arrangements to move to Minnesota, Luis Gustavo was being treated for Bell's palsy, a form of temporary facial paralysis resulting from damage or trauma to one of two facial nerves. The treatment, he remembers, was to apply electricity to the nerve in order to activate it. The final treatment was given about a week after my father went north. Then, we went for an airplane ride again and joined him at the Lauers.

About this time, and probably as a result of my brother's twisted mouth, I remember a porcelain statue of the Divine Infant Jesus of Prague appeared in our living room. I don't know who bought it, either Great-aunt Carmen or my mother, but it was dedicated to Luis. This is my first recollection of religious statuary in our home. My brothers and I wore gold chains with holy medals; mine bore the image of the Sacred Heart of Jesus.

My aunt and grandmothers were dedicated to the meditative practice of praying the rosary, so rosaries were familiar.

Meanwhile, other Cuban families who would be on the flight to Minnesota were preparing to move again.

Roberto and Noris Beruvides and their two children, José and Ariana, arrived in Miami from Havana on June 27, 1962. Initially, they moved into an apartment with one of Roberto's sisters, but it was crowded as other in-laws were living with her too. The Beruvides family transferred to an efficiency apartment on Flagler Avenue. Like most other refugees, they received a government subsidy and surplus food. Not long after their arrival, they understood Miami's predicament and therefore their own. Resettlement was the best option.

Consequently, the Beruvides family registered for relocation with Catholic Relief Services. San Francisco was Roberto's first choice. He hoped for opportunities in his profession: he was an actor. However, another family went. There were more willing sponsors with the Protestant congregations. Soon, a Presbyterian church in Philadelphia found sponsors. Everyone agreed to a September resettlement. But then Catholic Relief Services reported sponsorship available in St. Paul.

When Roberto brought home news of having found sponsorship in Minnesota, Noris agreed to resettle there. In a week's time they would leave the Miami apartment for the Twin Cities.

With a new destination in mind, Roberto went to the Cuban Refugee Center to select winter coats for his family. There, he met Hector San Domingo doing the same thing. They exchanged information about their families and their resettlement plans as they sifted through winter garments at the *Refugio*. Roberto said his wife, Noris, was petite so he was having trouble finding the right size coat. Hector said his wife, Manola, was also small.

They kept sorting through garments. Finally, each man decided on a coat for his wife, then lifted it to show one another the treasure. It was the exact same coat!

My father went to Miami International Airport to catch a Northwest Orient flight to the Twin Cities on August 30, 1962.

Besides being high season for hurricanes, late summer and early fall is a time of scorching heat in Miami. While waiting for the flight to board, my father met three other Cuban families who'd found sponsorship in Minnesota. They were Roberto and Noris Beruvides and their children José and Ariana. Hector and Manola San Domingo were ready with their daughter Ruth. Luis and Virginia Padilla had three boys, Luis, Eddie, and two-month-old Miami-born Miguel.

Luis Padilla was a lawyer in Havana, his wife, Virginia, a home economics teacher. They left Cuba for Miami in 1961 by way of a flight that stopped in Jamaica before coming to the United States. Virginia came a day before her husband. For one night, she stayed with an uncle in an apartment on Southwest Eighth Street. The following day, with help from the Catholic agency, she rented an apartment in the same building. Luis Padilla brought their two sons and soon found a job as a hotel bellboy, earning $30 a week.

The U.S. government had proposed resettlement to Minnesota. Sponsors were available in White Bear Lake. The Padillas had not considered resettlement. Today, Virginia (now Virginia Odio) is a snowbird who enjoys Miami winters and cooler Minnesota summers.

As these Cuban families waited to leave Miami, curious to learn more about his future home, my father approached an agent behind the airline counter. He asked about the current temperature in the Twin Cities.

"He said it was fifty-seven degrees. I went back to the group and said, 'You have sweated all you've sweated in your lives. You will never sweat again,'" my father said.

While everyone chuckled at his comments, I imagine the laughs were nervous ones.

The anecdote is an example of the belief system my father adopted: the past is over. It will never be again. Don't waste your time thinking about it. Don't talk about it, either. Why not? Because it doesn't exist.

How very Zen.

In her book *In the Land of Mirrors: Cuban Exile Politics in the United States,* Maria de los Angeles Torres writes about exiles and their relationship to memory. "Memory, remembering and re-creating become individual and collective rituals, as does forgetting."

Beyond the vital winter coats, I suspect staying warm was low on the Cuban list of concerns. At least initially. Employment, English skills, and good schools for the children were crucial.

There are many ways to process the traumatic loss of homeland, like the various ways people mourn a death. I know of a Cuban man who was practicing as a physician in Havana. After many years in exile in the Midwest, he lost the ability to speak Spanish, though comprehension remained. Some exiles were Creoles, that is, the first generation of Cubans born to Spaniards. They may have or do identify more closely with Spain. Many Cubans who resettled outside Miami encouraged their children to Anglicize their names to ease their way in the United States. Some people did not insist on their children speaking Spanish at home.

I don't know when it happened, but my mother became devoted to St. Jude, the patron of hopeless causes. Our family

was silent. Lips were sealed. Only when my maternal grandmother Manuela visited from Venezuela, always staying for several months, did I hear laments. Understandably, my parents
were annoyed with her voicing them. Keyed for survival, my
parents couldn't invest time or energy in what they considered
the luxury of mourning.

Cuban children had an easier time adapting to the new climate, though they struggled with restrictions arising from their
parents' fears. Many resettled Cubans lacked familiarity with so
many American behaviors. For example, my mother called my
brother inside the apartment the first time it snowed; she feared
he'd get sick.

I was too young to make comparisons about the weather
or our housing. I believed life was lived in numerous houses in
various climates because that's how we had lived. I didn't know
any other way.

Surely, the Cuban adults in Minnesota must have talked
among themselves. Were they sad when the days shortened and
the temperatures dropped below zero? Were they amazed with
their new wardrobes, which included unfamiliar items—long
underwear, boots, coats, scarves, hats, and gloves? Salting and
sanding sidewalks and entrances was a new practice. For those
who lived in houses with yards, what about that leaf raking
and burning?

I remember watching my father shovel the driveway. An
afternoon snow had fallen. It was dark. My mother's Buick was
inside the garage. He wore a wool coat, brim hat, and leather
gloves. I don't remember him laughing.

The adults in exile may have learned quickly what took me many
years and moves to learn. For one, the homeland is never forgotten, though many other places will be loved as home. A place

is called home, no matter where the dwelling is situated, for one reason: the sanctuary of home is carried within each person. The material manifestation of home—trailer, apartment, or mansion—is secondary.

The extended family is essential to Cubans. My mother's maternal aunt, Great-aunt Carmen, and her husband, Great-uncle Epifanio Echevarria, were with us from the beginning of exile. They moved from Miami to Minnesota and settled in the Sibley Manor Apartments in West St. Paul.

Their son, Dr. Orlando Echevarria, was my mother's first cousin, which in Spanish is *primo hermano*. The literal translation is brother-cousin, reminding everyone of the closeness of their relationship. When someone is identified as a first cousin, that person is announced as being loved in the same way we love our brothers and sisters. This love is a natural result of the love our parents had for their siblings. My mother's mother and Orlando's mother were the Spanish sisters.

Orlando, my mother, and her brother Homero were born and raised in Punta San Juan, Central Punta Alegre, Camaguey, a few houses from one another.

Starting in 1948, Orlando was in medical school at the University of Havana. However, in March 1952, the university closed as a consequence of a military coup d'état by a former Cuban president (1940–44) who had been living in Daytona Beach, Florida. Fulgencio Batista wanted to come back to Cuba in a big way. The 1952 elections were canceled. The United States supported this regime.

Consequently, in October 1953, Orlando left Cuba to finish medical school in Madrid, Spain. Two years later, he was in Ohio, working at a psychiatric hospital and studying for the U.S. medical boards. He married Carol Good, and eventually they had four children: Orlando Jr., Lisa, Victor, and Gina. Orlando obtained a license to practice medicine in the United States in 1966. The rest of his professional life was spent in Kankakee and Bourbonnais, Illinois.

My maternal grandmother Manuela Ballesteros González went into exile in May 1961 to Valencia, Venezuela. Her son Homero González was about to be married to an Italian-born immigrant to Venezuela, Antonietta Legrottaglie. In 1956, Homero had graduated as an electrical engineer from the University of Miami in Coral Gables, Florida. He traveled to New York City and attended a job fair where he learned Termec, S.A., had a position in Maracaibo, Venezuela. The company made an excellent offer and he moved.

Their three children are my first cousins, Patricia, Homero Alejandro, and Fabiola. Homero and Antonietta remained in Venezuela until they retired to Miami, Florida, in 2009.

From Venezuela, Grandmother Manuela visited Minnesota, as did my paternal grandparents Miguel and Evangelina Veiga. My maternal grandfather Severiano González stayed in Cuba and died there. No one in exile saw him again.

My father's only sibling, Rosita Veiga de Alvarez, and her husband, Rafael Alvarez, went into exile early in 1960 to Mexico City with their three children, my first cousins Rafael, Bernardo, and Lourdes.

Without a doubt, one impact of our resettlement in Minnesota was the family's faster rate of assimilation, especially on the part of the children. Due to the small numbers of Cubans in the Twin Cities, I suspect our assimilation was faster than for our counterparts who remained in Miami. There, Cuban cultural norms and Spanish language remained intact. The number of refugees in the community and waves of new ones reinforced Cuban traditions.

Our family was among the estimated 35 percent of the 165,000 Cubans who had registered at the Cuban Refugee Center who found new homes and work in places outside Miami by June 1963.

The experience of exile, especially during one's formative years, leaves an imprint. The constant moving to find a place to live then claiming many places as home does not let me forget that an exile is much of who I am.

"Once a refugee, always a refugee," writes Carlos Eire in his second book, *Learning to Die in Miami: Confessions of a Refugee Boy*, on his early exile as an unaccompanied child, one of more than fourteen thousand who were part of Operation Pedro Pan. While it is a hard truth, I like it. It's a bit of an affirmation.

"Where are you from?" I am asked, especially when I am north of Miami. To date, I have lived in Minnesota, Ohio, Virginia, Puerto Rico, and, briefly, in the Dominican Republic. My Florida homes include Miami, Coconut Grove, Homestead, and St. Augustine.

The question trying to place me typically surfaces after my first name has been said. Sometimes, we have pronunciation practice. I watch as people scan me physically for more information. There's confusion. My first answer is simple.

"It's a long story."

"What do you mean?"

"I'm a Cuban raised in Minnesota and Miami. I'm Cuban."

It's a long story. Do you have time?

Typically, people want to know more about Fidel or, in more recent years, about Raul Castro. Sometimes our information concerning what's transpiring in Cuba differs from what is gleaned from mainstream U.S. media reports. Cuban exiles listen to both English and Spanish media; news coverage of the island is crucial in Miami.

Besides, Cubans on both sides of the Florida Straits make and receive telephone calls, send letters and emails, and travel to and, more frequently now, from the island. The communication flows and recedes according to decrees by both countries.

My family's story, like that of many exiles, contains the elements of extraordinary loss—a severing from one's personal and collective history and homeland and the accompanying, often suppressed, grief. It is followed by some recovery—the increasing knowledge of different customs and the chance to participate as citizens of our adopted country. The story is laced with continuous ambiguity and high flexibility, states that, in time, become easier to tolerate. They are second nature to a person who is bicultural.

When we left Cuba, we weren't donning space suits or thinking ourselves explorers to the New World. Both of my parents had traveled to the United States before they married. My maternal grandfather, Severiano González, studied English and radio communications in Poughkeepsie, New York. One reason he didn't leave the island was because he didn't like the way of life he had known in the United States. He didn't want to join his only son and his family in Venezuela, either.

Bicultural lives are lived in the most unexpected places. It is my hope that native-born people of any country who have welcomed foreigners will benefit from the telling of the story of my family's early years in exile. Perhaps refugees, exiles, and immigrants—in spite of strange languages, foods, and customs—will not be such scary people. I hope more people will be moved to include them. I wish our hosts, now fellow citizens, would more vocally express what we brought and continue to bring to work sites, schools, churches and temples, and the larger U.S.

culture. And they won't have to name a celebrity like Gloria Estefan or Marco Rubio to do so.

When I idealize Cuba, I think of it as a place where my origins are never questioned. It's where my family, and therefore I, had a history. There, I would not fall under suspicion after an introduction or be invited to join something in order to fill a minority quota. In Cuba, people knew both sets of grandparents and maybe even their parents as decent, hardworking, family-oriented people. They had integrity. Most importantly, they were people with faith in God.

Unfortunately, an uninterrupted trajectory of relationships, generations of relationships with other families from birth to death, is impossible when one is in exile. In addition, the importance of place and one's relationship to it is corrupted. These are two of my major losses.

I would have liked to have known a life with continuity. The desire lingers from a natural flow's severance.

Many times when I've shared these longings, people shake their heads. They wonder if I've ignored the demographic changes that have transpired in the United States since World War II. Am I stuck watching reruns of Ozzie and Harriet?

The migratory pattern in the United States—from rural to urban, small town to big city, south to north, east to far west—is not news to me. Nomadic people and migration existed way before Europeans got on their boats and sailed west.

In *Goodhue County, Minnesota,* Fredrick L. Johnson writes about immigration to the United States during modern times. During the 156-year period from 1820 to 1975, at least 47 million immigrants reached America from countries around the world. About 13 million migrants between the years 1820 and 1950 returned to their native countries or moved to other nations. The percentage of returnees varied, with higher rates, for example, from Mediterranean Europe and lower ones for Scandinavia.

Those who returned to their country of origin were typically urban dwellers who did not own property or land.

In contrast to immigrants, political exiles lack choice about returning home. The expression of differing political beliefs might land them in jail. Unless they are crazy, why would they return to live in a place where dissidents are often silenced for expressing their views?

Minnesota is another home to me. If I hear a Minnesota accent in someone's English, it won't be long before I inquire about his or her relationship to the state.

I've had the pleasure of meeting three people who, unbeknownst to me, were sociolinguists. Their trained ears were working during chit-chat at an airport or banquet table. After a few minutes, they gingerly revealed conclusions: I'm a Latina from Minnesota. Amazing: I didn't have to explain a thing.

To this day, I am drawn to the quiet of the deep forests of northern Minnesota, where our family vacationed in lakeside cabins. I appreciate the freedom of playing and roaming outdoors without adult supervision. It has translated to my adult ability to explore wilderness areas for hours or to travel alone. I am blinded by the light of a cloudless winter day. I loved swimming in the river at Taylors Falls. These places are homes too, for they have provided me with beauty and comfort in various stages of my life.

In Minnesota, exposure to Norwegians and Germans was part of my formative years; as a result, it was natural to marry a man with both heritages. My husband is Richard Rettig of Seattle, Washington, whose mother, Mildred Januara Hegdahl, was a first-generation Norwegian Lutheran. His father, Roy Edward Rettig, was of German descent. Both of my brothers married midwestern women: Suzanne Barber and Marjorie MacArthur hail from Michigan.

Perhaps one cannot go home again, though often, in my mind and in my moves and travels, I kept trying.

It was a foolish practice. Which one would I return to, anyway?

Like hermit crabs, we exiles carry our homes with us. That is one of the major lessons of exile.

Blessed are the Chosen, for they shall always yearn for home, everywhere and nowhere in particular, and always find it in the most unusual places.

—Carlos Eire

CHAPTER 2

When Roberto and Noris Beruvides arrived at the airport in the Twin Cities, they were concerned. Their sponsors, Joe and Mary Jo Richardson, weren't there waiting for them. Instead, a woman from their parish greeted them and drove them to the Richardsons' home. The young couple waited there as they hadn't found a sitter for their children.

Roberto and Noris and their two children, José and Ariana, lived with the Richardsons temporarily. Noris Beruvides (now Noris Baldwin) remembered that sponsors met the other Cubans at the airport. Luis and Virginia Padilla and their boys went to White Bear Lake. Hector and Manola San Domingo and their daughter Ruth left with their sponsors.

These families and ours were among the 112 Cubans who had agreed to resettle in Minnesota by June 28, 1963. Others followed. Yet, during this first wave of exile—which began on January 1, 1959, and continued until the Cuban Missile Crisis on October 22, 1962—the numbers of Cubans who chose Minnesota as a place to resettle never swelled. At the zenith, about three hundred Cubans lived in the Twin Cities, according to my father.

The Cuban Refugee Center's resettlement office compiled a dossier for each family willing to relocate again, this time away from Miami. The dossiers included black-and-white photographs of family members and were distributed to interested congregations. Minnesotans who wanted to be of service by way of welcoming strangers could select a Cuban family to sponsor.

Like the other sponsors, Albert and Mernie Lauer knew quite a bit about my family and easily matched the photo of my father to the man arriving at the airport. At thirty-nine, Miguel Veiga was five foot seven and weighed 140 pounds. He was strong, as he lifted weights regularly. His hair was jet black with some baldness evident. His thin moustache was well groomed. Huge hazel eyes observed the world from behind dark-framed glasses. His nails were clean and buffed. His skin was as white as Casper the Friendly Ghost.

His sole suitcase went into the back of the Lauer's blue station wagon. The three headed to a reception at St. Peter's Catholic Church in Mendota Heights, where the Lauers were parishioners. St. Peter's is the oldest Catholic church in Minnesota, having been established in 1840. At the time of my father's arrival, Father Harvey F. Eagan was pastor. He had served the parish since 1957. He was the administrative liaison as well as the one who asked parishioners if they could find room in their hearts and hearths to help Cuban refugees.

The Lauers and my father went home to their farm after the reception. There, my father was pleased by and grateful for the comfortable basement lodgings. More than likely, he unpacked and then, as was his afternoon custom, showered. In time, he went upstairs to join the family for dinner.

Fortunately for us, my father's English was good, a result of early exposure to the language along with years of dedicated study. While managing a lumber business for his uncle, my father was an evening student at the University of Havana from 1940 to 1945.

My paternal grandparents, Miguel and Evangelina Veiga, had moved to Havana with him in order to help their son accomplish his educational goals. They rented a roomy upstairs apartment in the Vedado neighborhood on San Lazaro, an avenue that ends with the impressive steps of the University of Havana. He graduated from the university as a certified public accountant and also won two awards in English. During those student years he visited the Isle of Pines, now the Isle of Youth. The hotel registration transpired in English. Only in English.

English was part of his childhood. My great-aunts Andreita and Evelia, his mother's two older sisters, spoke it fluently. They learned while in elementary school on the Isle of Pines, which was under American occupation after the Spanish-American War. Schooling was in English.

Since 1895, Cuban nationalists had been fighting to gain independence from Spain. The U.S. occupation of Cuba began in April 1898 when the United States declared war on Spain. A few months later, in December 1898, the United States signed a peace treaty with Spain in Paris and took control of Cuba.

The Platt Amendment of 1901 established conditions the Cuban government had to agree to before U.S. forces would withdraw so Cuba could gain sovereignty, this time from the United States. One of the conditions was the United States giving up the Isle of Pines in exchange for an agreement to sell or lease territory for a naval base. That's how, in 1903, the United States got a lease for land to set up a naval base at Guantánamo.

Spanish returned to the classroom after the Platt Amendment went into effect. When my paternal grandmother Evangelina Monzón began elementary school on the Isle of Pines, classes were held in Spanish. As a result, she spoke only Spanish. Grand-mother Eva and her younger sister, my great-aunt Teté, never learned English, not even after forty-plus years in the United States. In Miami, the lack of English language skill is common. Their beloved brother, my great-uncle Luis, for whom my brother Luis Gustavo is named, remained in Cuba with his family.

My father's interest in learning a second language was born from listening to his aunts. Such early exposure allowed him insights into cultural differences that later, in exile, wouldn't be so foreign.

Still, it was inconceivable for him to envision his children becoming English dominant as a result of political exile.

The evening of my father's arrival in Minnesota, August 30, 1962, Al Lauer inquired about driving skills. No problem, my father said. To illustrate, he drove a Studebaker with a stick shift around the property for a little while. Al offered to loan him the car. The next day, with the joy of having three job interviews set and a map, my father drove into St. Paul. He accepted the most promising offer: assistant comptroller at Twin City Meats.

At first, my father commuted to work with a neighbor. Al Lauer explained the protocol of carpooling. My father would be a passenger contributing to gas costs. The arrangement was reasonable. He gladly gave the driving neighbor twenty-five cents in the morning and twenty-five cents for the return trip to Mendota Heights after work.

When he returned from the office, he showered to be refreshed for dinner. Every evening he ate upstairs with the Lauers. They enjoyed trading stories. Until his wife and children arrived the following week, he went downstairs and to bed early, he said, as after-dinner activities were limited.

Not long after starting at Twin City Meats, my father went into city hall on company business. There, he was pleased to find a bronze bust of the great Cuban patriot José Martí. The independence leader was easily identifiable by his receding hairline and copious moustache. In 1895, Martí was killed in the battle of Dos Ríos during the island's fight for independence from Spain.

The Cuban government had given the bust to St. Paul native Robert Butler, who was the U.S. ambassador to Cuba from June 1948 to February 1951. The Butler family gave it to the city so it would be displayed in a place of prominence. That is how a bust of Cuba's national hero—on both sides of the Florida Straits— came to be located in the north end staircase lobby of city hall in downtown St. Paul. Martí has been in this spot since 1994, his third place in the building.

I am sure my father found some comfort in seeing the bust, for José Martí had been an exile in the United States too. During the late 1800s, the patriot organized, wrote, and raised funds in the United States, working for Cuban independence.

For a decade, I have lived in St. Augustine, Florida, a place that was once Spanish territory controlled from Havana. Next to the Cathedral Basilica on the plaza, there is a bronze statue of the Cuban Father Félix Varela. He is a fellow political exile and on the road to canonization. Varela went to New York City. Aside from being a missionary priest to Irish immigrants, he was an intellectual grandfather to José Martí and other Cuban patriots. He died in 1853, the year José Martí was born.

The bronze stands in the very spot where Varela died. The saintly scholar and independence leader lived here. I connect to my island heritage from here. This thread, somehow, provides a little comfort. I am in sync with other Cuban exiles who lived here before me.

When you live outside your country of origin, historical continuity takes on more importance. Consider the U.S. expatriate communities in London or Paris or Mexico or Costa Rica.

George Heimel, the owner of Twin City Meats, a Catholic of German descent, decided to improve my father's life by providing him with more independence. He bought my father a car, a Mercury, for $500. It ended the carpooling arrangement, though my father had been comfortable with it. He repaid Heimel on a monthly basis.

One major contribution my father made to Twin City Meats during his tenure involved cost accounting. The company did not price meat in a profitable manner. For example, my father explained, if the company bought a cow for $500, it was butchered and the company sold the parts for the same cost per pound. However, not all cuts of beef carry the same value in the marketplace. Soup bones aren't as valuable as filet, he reasoned. So he found a good reference book on cost accounting, one published in Chicago. Then he devised a formula to determine what the real profits were when livestock was bought, butchered, and sold on the wholesale market.

In time, no doubt as a result of my father's good working relationship with the company's comptroller, Joseph Wiblishauser, our family was invited to his home. The rare social invitation raised eyebrows and curiosity at the office.

Wiblishauser was an avid birdwatcher, an enemy of communism, and a religious man. I remember my first visit to his lakeside home in Wisconsin. The house was on a hillside but I didn't know it. The foyer was at ground level, but then we went down a few steps. I imagined finding a dark, damp basement.

Instead, I was delighted. The lower level held a family room with a huge picture window. I remember the comfort of that room—the wood paneling, the fireplace, the sofa. I remember the dark green of the pine trees and the lake beyond them.

One day, George Heimel asked my father to accompany him to the bank. There, he introduced my father and explained that he had earned the privilege of signing company checks and borrowing up to $50,000 without obtaining permission.

At the time my father wondered, how is it that this man trusts me? As far as he knows, I'm a Cuban refugee without any assets. My father was amazed at the confidence and trust shown by people who hadn't known him or his family his entire life. That would *not* have been the norm in Cuba.

Eventually, Mr. Wiblishauser retired. When he did, he recommended my father take his position.

That is how, late in 1965, after almost four years with the company, my father became its comptroller. My parents bought their first home in the United States in suburban Roseville. We were learning English. Other Cuban families were in town. Often, we visited at one another's houses and celebrated more formally at the International Institute. Our friendship with the Lauer family deepened. Life moved in a good direction.

The Lauer family witnessed our many moves. Two years later, in 1968, they faced one of their own. They were forced to sell their farm in Mendota Heights as Interstate 35E was drawn through their property. Years passed before the project was completed. They moved to a three hundred–acre farm south of Rosemount.

But that autumn when our family arrived, these facts were in the undecipherable future. My parents kept their minds on God and on daily concerns.

Those were enough to keep them busy. My mother spoke some English when she came to the United States, as she had studied it throughout her schooling, including at the university level. However, her English language skills needed improvement. In a few months, she was expecting a fourth child. She needed to learn to drive and to cook. She would manage a household without extra hands, though her mother and aunt contributed greatly to its functioning. Fortunately, in Minnesota she didn't have to immediately work outside the home to generate income—there was enough work with three children and a baby on the way while adjusting to a new way of life.

"They're not going to adjust to us; we have to adjust to them," she once told my father. For many years, that was true.

Some adjustments to U.S. norms are easier to incorporate than others. Tolerance is needed in some cases. Rejection is called for in others. Some adaptations are seamless, automatic. Other ways are adopted after much thought. Such is the process of assimilation.

Meanwhile, my father began to see that the grass in Minnesota was signaling a change.

For one thing, the dandelions were going to seed. While they brightened the summer lawns with yellow flowers, in Minnesota they are considered weeds destined for removal. Their flowers became ghostly tufts. The Lauer children taught us to pick one and hold it gingerly by the stem. Then, we were to make a wish and blow the tuft. Seeds dispersed like tiny parachutes.

A second sign appeared one morning. Al Lauer called my father to a window. The morning dew on the lawn had turned to frost.

It was early September.

For the Lord, your God, is the God of gods, the Lord of lords, the great God, mighty and awesome, who has no favorites, accepts no bribes, who executes justice for the orphan and the widow, and befriends the alien, feeding and clothing him.

—Deuteronomy 10:17

CHAPTER 3

A Minnesota September is characterized by temperature fluctuations. When summer skies dominate, they are periwinkle with a few white clouds. Many days and even nights are hot and humid, evidence that summer wants to linger. Sometimes it rains. The leaves begin trading their greens for other colors. Cooler breezes nudge in. A few nights might dip into the high thirties, a taste of coming winter.

My mother, siblings, and I arrived in the Twin Cities during this transitional time, September 1962.

The new man and woman who didn't speak Spanish—I don't recall meeting them until we got to their house. In the foyer of their home I learned Albert and Mernie, generous souls, were our sponsors. The two had met at church bible study. Mernie was a Lutheran who became a Catholic. They married in 1941. For them, home was their farm at 2450 Lexington Avenue in Mendota Heights, sixty acres, theirs since 1952. Now they shared it with foreigners.

Albert was an engineer who built greenhouses for a living, as the founder, owner, and operator of Albert J. Lauer, Inc. Mernie managed the household.

Mr. Lauer's business office was on the premises, inside a big red barn. We stayed away from the office unless he waved us inside. Sometimes, he kept materials for the business stored in the barn. Other times, hay was piled, stacked, or strewn on the floor and in the loft.

The barn was exciting! Without parents watching, Luis Gustavo jumped from the loft into hay. The bolder Lauer kids dove from the loft, belly-flopping into the hay below.

In Mr. Lauer's office, there was a coffeemaker and sugar cubes for the coffee. We were from a land of sugar but had not seen it in cubes. How did that happen? How odd. Al taught Luis to feed sugar cubes to the horse, palm open, and to scatter corn for the chickens. A sow lived in a nearby pen and she scared my brother, so he left her alone.

Perhaps it was Al Lauer's aquarium that impressed Luis with its angled stainless steel frame so heavily glued. A sixty-watt light bulb warmed its water and gave light to the fish and aquarium plants. Guppies lived there. From a young age, Luis Gustavo had a penchant for breeding fish, fresh and salt-water. Even as an adult, he continues to breed and sell them.

I was four years old when we arrived that September in 1962. In less than two months, on November 1, All Saints' Day, I'd turn five. The Roman Catholic Church celebrates that day as a Holy Day of Obligation, since it marks the closing of the Easter season. Saints, known and unknown, are honored. One of my childhood playmates, Ed Lauer, is now in his early sixties and runs the family business. Recently, we shared a meal and conversation at his home in Farmington, Minnesota. It was only then that I learned his late father and I share a birthday. The continuity of this connection pleases me.

Sharecroppers farmed the remaining Lauer acreage. They grew corn, oats, alfalfa, and soybeans. In return, the family received one-third of the crop as payment, according to Joe Lauer, the eldest son, who was away at college when we occupied his family's basement.

Was it strange to him that a Cuban refugee family was coming to live there?

"No, not at all," he said without missing a beat. "We had the room. The basement had been used by us before as living quarters. A family needed a place to stay for a while and that was fine."

The sounds of greetings near the door, the moving of suitcases, I hear those in my memory. However, I don't see us going downstairs to our new residence. We must have done so because soon, I recall, we went upstairs to meet the rest of the Lauer family.

The Lauer family had nine children—Joe, Mary, Jane, Kathy, Ed, Michael, Marty, Ruth, and Dorothy, the youngest, born in 1960. Introductions were efficient. The two families lined up and faced one another. The Lauer children who were present assembled according to height, more or less. My heart sang "Let's play!" when I saw the number of children who were potential friends.

Our first American friends accepted us in a snap. They didn't speak Spanish. Ruth, a year older than I, became my closest friend. I didn't speak English. Luis Gustavo, having gone to first grade in Miami, spoke a little. Yet the lack of a common language didn't stop the Lauers and Veigas from becoming playmates. Of the Lauer children, Luis Gustavo later said, "Anybody was your friend."

Our younger brother, blond-haired Juan Carlos, was about to turn three. He wasn't speaking any language. There was concern, not alarm, among the adults about this. They concluded he was hearing and absorbing two languages. Out loud, the adults said he was confused about which to speak.

Over the years, I watched the Lauer children do things around the house and farm that my brothers and I never did. For example, the business of completing chores was a phenomenon I watched with interest. The children had household chores; their level of difficulty was assigned by age. Straightening their bedrooms—making the beds, picking up clothes and toys—were regular tasks. Helping with the dishes—washing and drying them and setting the table—were others.

When those were done, other chores waited around the property.

"Every day, twice a day, one of my jobs was to milk the cows. It's funny, as soon as I left for college, and my dad had to do the milking, he got rid of the cows," said Joe Lauer.

Many adult hands worked in our household, with my great-aunt, mother, and sometimes grandmother Manuela around for many months. Our main role was to obey our elders, not just our parents. The Lauer children had to do the same. However, for us, chores were not part of obedience. We paid attention to directions from our elders and excelled in our schoolwork. That went without saying.

In fact, we did not have chores until later, when my brothers were old enough to push a lawn mower and empty garbage cans. Reading trumped chores. If on a Saturday morning my mother found me reading a book in bed, she left me alone with it until later in the day. When I was fifteen, my mother took a part-time job in order to gather enough hours to sit for an exam so she could work as an optician. I agreed to clean house, but she paid me $5 to do so.

As a result of our special guest status, I remember the sixty-acre farm as a place of pleasure. There was room to run with boys and girls of all ages, a place to discover what else was new. When one is young, everything is new. It's especially true if one's address keeps changing. In our case, we were engaged in adapting to a dramatically different climate with four seasons, not the two seasons of the subtropics, and learning a new language.

Rogers Lake on the southwestern corner of the Lauers' property is the location of some of my best memories with the family. It was a place to cool off in the summer, but better still, when winter came, the soft slopes around the lake were excellent for sledding. One of the Lauer boys taught us how to identify where the ice was thin—he warned about the danger of cracking ice and freezing water. I learned to ice skate hanging on to the back of a chair once an area on the lake was cleared of snow.

I sat on the ground and unbuckled my boots, then pulled on a borrowed pair of white, somewhat scuffed leather skates. These had come down the line from the older Lauer girls. I tightened the laces. Urged on by Ruth or one of her brothers, I learned to ice skate before learning to speak English.

Once, using gestures, one of the older Lauer boys asked if I wanted to ride the horse. I nodded. He lifted me onto what was to me a strange, huge animal. He didn't take its lead and walk it, but let me sit there to get the feel of what it was like to sit on a horse.

New animals, surroundings, people, these novelties appealed to me. The quality of natural light in our new basement home was also different. I looked up to see natural light coming in through small windows lacking curtains. This was different from the windows of the other places we'd lived. One couldn't control the little light coming into the living area, where my brothers and I slept.

I longed for more light. The sunlight in Cuba and Miami is so strong that shades are pulled or louvers lowered on certain windows to keep it out. One works to cool the house. In northern climates, people want more sunlight to warm them, but drapes are often drawn to keep the heat inside. Especially during the middle of the day in a subtropical summer, the sunlight is harsh and dulls colors with its whitening effect.

My parents' bedroom was separate from the living area. The bathroom was roomy—I remember taking a shower there and pulling the large curtain across it. There was no tub.

Juan Carlos remembers the large shower stall and dripping showerhead. He also recalls feeling abandoned when he was left alone in the basement.

"I remember being down there, but I didn't know I was living there," said Luis Gustavo about our first home in Minnesota. He was confused by so many moves under his belt by age seven.

We ate meals upstairs with the Lauers. My first American meals were at their table. Luis recalls Mernie's meatloaf, accompanied by mashed potatoes and fresh peas. It is doubtful we'd eaten fresh peas before arriving in Minnesota. Canned green peas, yes. Because of Cuba's proximity to the United States, by the 1950s the country's cuisine had adopted many canned foods and condiments. Early canned peas sprinkle many Cuban yellow rice dishes, fricassees, and stews.

Mernie's meatloaf still defines American comfort food for my older brother. When Luis craves it, though he is a good cook, he asks his American wife, Suzi, to make it.

"I tried to get Mom to replicate it but she never could," Luis said.

Of course, only Cuban comfort food suffices at other times. I wonder what situations trigger each preference.

His comment doesn't surprise me. Our mother was not a skilled cook because she was not encouraged to become one. I can see various women and girls in the Lauer kitchen, cleaning up after dinner. My mother was probably among them, helping clear the table or dry dishes. She might have timidly asked questions about the meal, inquiring how a particular dish was cooked, though her natural interest was minimal. For refugees and immigrants, to follow real interests is a luxury; for her, doing so was no longer relevant.

Certainly, the taste of farm-fresh vegetables and eggs must be celebrated.

However, our palates were used to Cuban seasonings. The foundation of Cuban cuisine involves a sauté called a *sofrito*. Everyday dishes are built using the basics of olive oil, onion, garlic, and green pepper, and sometimes tomato sauce.

Scholarship was more important than cooking skills in my family, though this may defy some people's view of Latinas. Likewise, my great-aunt Carmen, an excellent seamstress who would be recognized today as a textile artist, refused to teach my sister Glenna or me to sew.

She shook her head no when I asked.

"Study hard so you can work and pay the seamstress," she said, after taking the pins out of her mouth. I stood on a wooden box where she could more easily mark the hemline on a new wool dress for me.

Like that of the Latino lover, Cuban women's culinary expertise is another myth. Poor cooking skill is not uncommon among women of my mother's generation. They were encouraged and able to further their formal education.

My maternal grandparents encouraged my mother's studies since she showed capacity for it. She responded. She was educated for her own sake but also for the good of the larger family. Her earning power improved with a university education. In an extended family, members help one another, especially because of their physical proximity. Many generations share one roof in exile and in Cuba.

In contrast, many American children travel miles, even to another part of the country, for an annual visit to their grandparents' house. Cuban children take fewer trips to visit their elders since they are often living in the same house. A carport is easily converted into an efficiency apartment for the grandparents. I knew a Cuban girl who shared a house with both sets of grandparents. I admire their ability to manage all those relationships! This tradition helped Cuban exiles gain economic security for themselves rather quickly.

In *Miami: City of the Future*, T. D. Allman explains that inadvertently, Fidel Castro contributed to the exile community's success by his immigration strategy. Fidel stopped military-age men from leaving the country. Meanwhile, he encouraged those considered "unproductive" to make their way elsewhere. These included young women, unattached mothers, and older people. As a result, Cuban immigration differs from that of other Latin American countries as women outnumber the men, especially single men.

This particular plan translated into having extra hands helping to run exile households. Childcare, cleaning, cooking, and laundry, typically women's work, was distributed. The woman head of household often found paid work. Or, if the woman sewed, she might have stayed home and completed piecework for local factories.

It is a rare Cuban, or perhaps an assimilated one, who subscribes to the do-it-yourself philosophy that reigns in the United States. There is no shame involved in hiring someone to help you. Doing so does not reflect on one's abilities or morality. Paying for a service, whether it's lawn care, ironing, weekday meal delivery, or housekeeping, is a positive. One eases one's load while creating jobs for others. The community is important, not just one's pride in self-reliance or an enhanced bank account.

Some Minnesotans did not know Cuba's geographic location and asked my parents to describe it. Since the starting point of their knowledge was so elementary, my parents understood it would be a difficult undertaking to explain themselves and the rest of our ways.

In Cuba, my mother, Maria Severiana González Ballesteros, became a doctor of pharmacy and of optometry, graduating with two degrees from the University of Havana. To be closer to her family, she opened a business as an optometrist. She rented the front rooms of a house in Caibarién, Cuba.

Luis Monzón owned the house. He was my paternal grand-mother's sole brother. My great-uncle Luis eventually intro-duced his tenant to his nephew, my father. My parents courted in Caibarién, but the wedding was in a Catholic church near the university in Havana.

In the United States, my mother's professional training had little relevance. It belonged to the past. In order to work as an optometrist or pharmacist, she needed to have a U.S. license. To get one, she would have to take and pass professional exams in English. Before sitting for one of them, she needed a num-ber of hours of work in the field. Her English skills needed improvement. In short, when we arrived in the Twin Cities, she might have been seen as a liability—a married refugee with some English, a mother of three due to give birth again in a few months' time.

After three weeks at the Lauers, we packed our suitcases and moved to the Sibley Manor complex in West St. Paul. A small group of Cubans rented there. Al Lauer and my father had gone to see the apartments. My father rented a two-bedroom basement unit there in a building near the river. The Padilla, San Domingo, and Beruvides families who had been on the flight with my father became neighbors.

From there, we children had joyful visits with the Lauers. We had little, if any, adult supervision outdoors. We ran and played everywhere. There were many children who could race to the house for help from an adult if we got into trouble.

"We had fun, didn't we?" asked Ed Lauer, who was ten years old when we met.

"Yes, we did," I said.

We smiled across the living room of his house in Farmington, Minnesota.

To avoid being called to complete chores, the Lauer children kept busy playing, he said.

Such freedom to explore is one reason for the hold wide-open spaces have on me. I am attracted to woods, lakes, streams, oceans, quarries, plains, saw grass prairies, tidal marshes, beaches, coral reefs, as well as farmers' fields. The outdoors, especially if the area is sparsely populated, offers solace. There, I go for the deepest silence to make myself available to hear God's voice.

For many years, I was a cultural Catholic, that is, a nonpracticing Catholic. I believed in God but instead of going to Mass, I sought natural places for the comforts of solitude, reflection, and prayer. I met others like me. I also met former Catholics who'd become agnostic or atheist yet claimed cultural Catholicism. Others engaged in Buddhist meditation to complement a yoga practice.

The Benedictine monk Laurence Freeman gave a talk about meditation at a local Catholic retreat center a few years ago. Fortunately, I attended, though I knew nothing about him. He founded the World Community for Christian Meditation. Freeman gave a great talk, introducing me to the practice of Christian meditation as taught by the late Benedictine monk John Main. Every morning I begin again with this form of prayer.

As a practicing Catholic for many years again, I am invigorated by Pope Francis. The gentle, loving man brings new energy to the Roman Catholic Church in every nation. In particular, Latin Americans hold him close to their hearts.

His second encyclical, *Laudato Si'*, is the first devoted to the environment. In it, Pope Francis calls for every person—not just Catholics—to examine their conscience in order to see the role he or she plays in caring for our common home.

The Fourth of July parties were festive at the Lauer farm. The picnic tables were covered with checkered tablecloths and laden with food. Every family brought a dish to share. My father could still list many of the families who attended, thanks to his excellent memory, even into his nineties.

"Al had nine children. His brother Gerald had thirteen. Another brother John had four. We had four. The piano teacher and her husband came with their eight children," he said. "We always brought Cuban black beans and rice to eat with the hot dogs and hamburgers and corn."

Our families cultivated friendship. Albert and Mernie Lauer agreed to be my sister's godparents. Glenna was born in February 1963 and named after Mernie's sister, Glenna Kerker van Keuran, partly as a way of honoring that new friendship. The van Keurans lived in St. Paul.

By the time we met Glenna, she was divorced and her children were grown. The oldest son, Bob, had begun minor seminary studies. We'd see him during the holidays. He spoke some

Spanish so we warmed to him. Tom studied engineering at the University of Minnesota. Carol was institutionalized due to severe Down syndrome. Glenna supported the family by working as a bookkeeper. In addition, she painted in a variety of mediums.

On the weekends when the weather was good, she set up an easel at Como Park Zoo. She sketched charcoal portraits for extra income.

I liked Glenna. She had a round face and wore gold-framed glasses. Her skin was very fair and she had black hair. When I was in third or fourth grade, she encouraged my writing, giving me a diary with a lock and key. The gift introduced me to privacy as well as to the importance of documenting my thoughts and experiences.

Yet I had questions about Glenna that, when answered, caused distress. Where was her husband? He left, someone said. Where is her daughter? She's in a state hospital. Why? No answer. Bob came and went. Where did he go? To the seminary, someone said. He's studying.

Her family's model was so different from the one Glenna's sister Mernie Lauer or my mother had: husband and children. Why were those key people missing from her home? My grandmother's husband was in Cuba. That was strange. But I knew where he was. Glenna lived with her mother and that made sense. My great-aunt or grandmother or mother were always home.

In turn, Minnesotans had questions about Cuban ways. Bob van Keuran said one Cuban family in his parish revealed that on weekends, the parents let the children climb into bed with them.

"This astounded Minnesotans," he said.

Luis Gustavo was a lot of fun to talk to, Bob said, though at first he didn't want to speak English.

"You didn't either," he said.

A few short years passed and I wouldn't speak Spanish with Bob.

The Minnesota accent was hard for my father to decipher.

"Of all of you, Joe is the most difficult to understand," Joe Lauer recalled my father saying to him.

When my father asked Joe to repeat what he'd said, Joe paraphrased his words.

"That probably made it worse, now that I think of it," Joe Lauer said.

In turn, my father's accent and expressions were strange to Ed Lauer, who was ten years old when they met.

"My dad would ask Miguel if he wanted a drink, a beverage or a beer or something. Your father would reply, 'I'm fine,'" said Ed Lauer.

The boy thought it was an odd way to say, "No, thank you."

While some cultures prefer direct response to questions, other cultures believe such honesty is rude. For a Cuban to give quick "No, thanks" to an offer is considered curt. I learned to wait for two offers from a host before accepting what he or she offered.

"Want a Coke?"

"No, thank you."

"Are you sure? I know you like it."

"Okay, thank you."

Nuances and patterns like these take time to understand and identify. A poet friend, a Midwesterner, married a Cuban exile; they had two children. The family lived in Spain and in Miami. She worked hard to become bilingual and bicultural. She is an American-Cuban. They're around.

"Whenever a Cuban says '*Sí, sí, sí, sí, sí*' really fast, what the person really means is no," she said.

I laughed. She's right.

Our names took on new manifestations in the mouths of Minnesotans. Four syllables in Marisella! My mother named me for a character in a classic Venezuelan novel. Using a middle name wasn't an option. It is Lourdes, after the place in France where the Virgin Mary appeared. In Spanish it is pronounced "Lur Des." My name can't shrink to one syllable.

Glenna's name is bilingual. Maria is her middle name. Marisella is a variation of Mary. Our mother was Maria Severiana, her mother Maria Manuela, her aunt Maria del Carmen. The Blessed Mother is never forgotten. We carry her name, although I don't recall anyone having a special devotion to Mary.

One of my favorite prayers is from the opening lines of Mary's canticle: "My soul magnifies the Lord, and my spirit rejoices in God my Savior. For He who is mighty has done great things for me, and holy is His name."

Indeed the Lord has done great things for me. High on the list is the generosity of the Lauer family. They responded to the directions of His spirit. They befriended and sheltered us, aliens.

I like to think that when we left their house for the next one, we were a little less foreign to them, and they to us.

We packed the Mercury and moved to Sibley Manor at the end of September. My brothers and I shared the backseat of the car, talking as we drove to our next home. Our parents explained our great-aunt and uncle were living right above us.

By the end of the month, pumpkins were stacked outside the doors of grocery stores. They huddled underneath the tables of roadside vegetable stands. Soon they'd be hollowed out and sport carved faces for Halloween. Their flesh would be spiced and baked into muffins and pies. We learned about and joined in those harvest activities.

Elementary school classes had begun. Soon we'd draw attention to ourselves as latecomers, Spanish-onlys, dark ones—for heaven's sakes, Cubans!

The Lauer farm was the fifth place I'd lived in my four-year-old life. I had lived in two countries with two languages. While such changes early in life teach a child flexibility, their regularity created problems.

As the moves took place during my formative years, they contributed to a template of displacement and starting over that became standard, a pattern.

The template had rules. It demanded I abandon a situation for another in order to improve my life. Negotiation didn't exist. Compromise was impossible. Only severance solved a problem. This particular mindset is needed when a person prepares to go into exile. Go or stay. Conform or keep quiet. However, the model loses its value when one is later confronted with job difficulties or relationship problems. Go or stay is not as productive in those instances.

I was as powerless to change this approach to living as I had been unable to stop any of the moves as a child. Later, my father acknowledged that both he and my mother were concerned about the impact. I thought they didn't care about the difficulties we faced, especially at school. They never spoke of it.

Each move had benefits. Even as a toddler in Cuba, I liked variety in toys. The move north offered a brand-new environment and language. Those challenges were enough. The trading of one thing for another and making choices is implicit in variety. However, our experience with it involved regular losses, beloved people and places we could not recuperate. We were not taught how to mourn these losses.

So it was only natural for me to see the superficial roots I grew when it came to settling in one place. Any wind caused this seedling to fly off and land elsewhere for a short time. I sought better work, true love, or cheaper housing.

Finally, in my mid-thirties, I was eager for deeper roots. A faculty job at the Homestead Campus of Miami Dade Community College provided much-needed financial stability. I bought a small house in that farming community a few years after it had recovered from Hurricane Andrew.

A certain sense of homelessness ended with the purchase.

One of the first trees I planted in my backyard was an African tulip tree. I fell in love with its canopy and red-orange blooms in Puerto Rico. I wanted a physical reminder of that much-loved island, so I spent $100 on the tree.

One day during hurricane season, high winds crossed South Florida. They knocked down the tree. After the storm passed, I surveyed the yard for damages. The tree lay on the grass like a corpse. My heart sank. I called a nurseryman friend.

"You can save it," he said. "Prop it back up with some rope and put boards around it."

"I don't know," I said.

"Look, that tree has superficial roots. They'll never break the limestone. Think about how you swung that pickax to plant your fruit trees," he said.

The tree's response to future storms was predictable. No matter how gorgeous its blooms, I didn't want to continue the template. Like Cuba, like everywhere else I'd lived, Puerto Rico would stay alive in my memory and imagination.

I'd had enough of temporary. Easily, I gave the tree away.

The author's first grade photograph at St. Mark's Catholic School

Maria Severiana González de Veiga is ready for winter.

Left to right, back: Great-uncle Epifanio Echevarria, Great-aunt
Carmen Echevarria, Miguel Veiga. Front: the author and brother
Juan Carlos

Marisella and Juan Carlos on a Dayton Avenue sidewalk

Author and brother Luis Gustavo at the Lauer house

Veiga family in Miami, Christmas Day, 1961, almost a year after arriving from Cuba

Center: Albert J. Lauer, our sponsor, on the Lauer farm in Mendota Heights; Great-uncle Epifanio to his right (Photo credit: courtesy of the Lauer family)

Picnic at the Lauers', July 1963 (Photo credit: courtesy of the Lauer family)

Luis, Glenna, Juan Carlos, Grandmother Manuel, and me

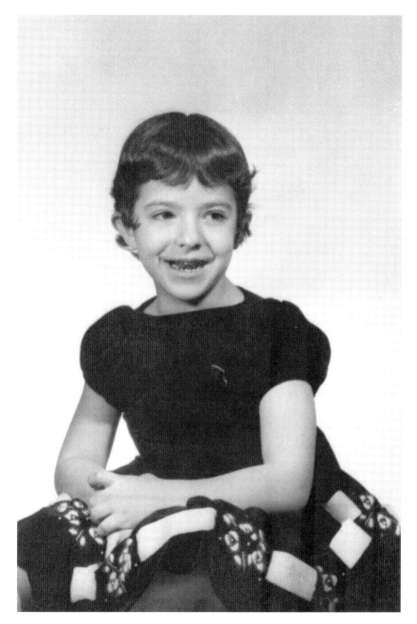

Glenna Maria, born in St. Paul, Minnesota

Lunch at home restaurant in Batabanó, Cuba (Photo credit: Tina Bucuvalas)

Veiga house on the hill in Cojímar (Photo credit: Raul Arcia)

Living room, Veiga house in Cojímar (Photo credit: Raul Arcia)

To live is to sink roots. Life is possible only to the extent that you find a place hospitable enough to receive you and allow you to settle down. What follows is a sort of symbiosis: Just as you grow into the world, the world grows into you. Not only do you occupy a certain place, but that place, in turn, occupies you.

—Costica Bradatan in "The Wisdom of the Exile," *New York Times,* August 16, 2014

CHAPTER 4

In addition to her roles as baby and princess, for years my sister Glenna starred as the sole blood relative born in the United States. Glenna, *la americana*. From St. Luke's Hospital in February 1963, she went to the Sibley Manor apartment complex in West St. Paul. Our 730-square-foot basement apartment was one of five hundred fifty units in fifty-five buildings on twenty-two acres of land. Other Cubans had moved to ten-year-old Sibley Manor as well.

Then and now, the Julen family owned and operated the apartment complex. To their credit, they have stayed true to their founding mission, which is to provide clean, safe, and affordable housing. Originally, the Julens had military housing in mind—specifically, Korean War veterans and people working at nearby Fort Snelling, according to *Community Reporter* editor Jerry Rothstein. Those populations declined during the late 1950s. Airline and airport workers followed as tenants.

The Beruvides family moved from their sponsors' house to an apartment inside an old, divided house on Rice Street. The living quarters were small, with one bathroom and a master bedroom. The children, José and Ariana, shared a room with many windows behind the kitchen, probably a sun porch.

The Beruvides family was not satisfied with their new place, partly stemming from living apart from other Cubans. At the time, many Cubans gathered at the St. Paul home of an American woman who had sponsored an exile family. Roberto Beruvides went to see her about moving again, this time to Sibley Manor.

The Beruvides family moved to an apartment facing a court-yard in the 1358 building and it was their home for many years. Luis Padilla helped with the physical move. Already, his wife, Virginia, and their three boys were settled at Sibley Manor.

Meanwhile, some Minnesotans were not pleased with our coming into the United States. A December 5, 1965, *Minneapolis Tribune* article, "Public Uneasy over Influx of Cubans," gives the results of a statewide poll concerning Cuban immigration. "A majority of the people taking part in a statewide survey (51 percent) think the United States should NOT encourage Cuban families to leave their homeland."

Minnesotans were "just as reluctant about inviting Cuban families to live in Minnesota. Fifty-two percent believe it would be a 'poor idea' to invite Cuban families to settle in their communities, while 34 percent look upon that as a good idea."

The arguments against our immigration still echo today. The opposition said we'd work for lower wages and therefore hijack jobs from American workers; they said the United States could not afford to care for more people, Cubans wouldn't adapt to a different social structure; Communists and other troublemakers would be among the refugees. Adaptation to the climate was another reason.

The Beruvides family underwent many changes in order to adapt quickly to their new home in Minnesota. Roberto Beruvides had been a professional actor in Cuba. In the Twin Cities, he worked two jobs, one with EMC, on equipment; another involved making Spanish language recordings. Later, Roberto worked at a factory during the day, with my uncle Epifanio. Roberto's evening job was at KTCA television. Noris also used her Spanish language skills to make recordings. In addition, she provided childcare in their apartment. Eventually, Noris went to cosmetology school to become a licensed hairdresser.

Like other Cubans, their household furnishings were sparse and rickety, Noris said. The double bed, for example, was missing a leg so she and her husband propped it up with brick. When they moved to Sibley Manor, the bricks were accidentally left on Rice Street. They discovered this, much to their dismay, when they were exhausted from moving and setting up the bed. Quickly, the bricks were replaced.

My great-uncle Epifanio had been referred to a thrift shop for second-hand furniture. Refugees were directed there in order to make selections suitable for their household. He was amazed by the inventory in the warehouse.

"I've never seen such a large collection of garbage," he told my father.

From those stacks of rejected furniture, unmatched plates, and tired clothing, we initially set up households.

We were grateful. My family is not pretentious. However, the underlying message tied like a little price tag to every second-hand item was this: be satisfied with leftovers.

Owning used goods does not constitute a character flaw. It becomes problematic when others associate it with being people who are less moral, less worthy, perhaps even less human.

Those early days in Minnesota resurfaced when I was in my mid-twenties. I was living in Toledo, Ohio. I'd just gotten a master's degree. I was teaching as an adjunct professor and writing. Two of my poems had been published in an important journal edited by Ireland's best poet, Seamus Heaney. Though low on income and without a car, I was healthy. I lived in a cool (also read: poorly insulated) Victorian house with other young people. My free time was spent with other poets and visual artists. Toledo has a tradition of good live jazz. I didn't go to church on Sundays; instead, I walked a few blocks to the art museum and spent time before favorite paintings.

That day, I sifted through used women's clothing at a thrift shop in downtown Toledo. More than likely, I was searching for sweaters, as my winter wardrobe was and remains limited. I heard a foreign language. The voices belonged to a Vietnamese family—a mother, an older woman who could have been her mother, and two children. Rack by rack, they sought inexpensive, warm clothing.

The Vietnamese family was a painful reminder of my early years. I knew their purpose in the store. That was us, I thought. It was the first time I felt such a powerful link to my childhood experience.

The moment was overwhelming. So was the aftermath of depression. The days of early exile in this country, those days were never the subject of my writing. I focused on learning technique and craft in my poetry. Like many women writers before me, I explored the private worlds of family, love, and sometimes nature. These worlds provide fodder. In my early forties, I began writing commentary on the U.S. Hispanic experience for Hispanic Link News Service. I danced around many key topics.

The public world of politics was dangerous. It was traumatic for our family; therefore, I avoided it. Yet I couldn't deny that a political revolution had redirected our lives. Writing about exile was tricky as a result of its triumphs but also its inherent cultural conflicts. I also lacked the confidence to be honest with readers.

So many of my thoughts were hidden or ignored, just as my elders deleted our past life in Cuba. A blank past was a coping mechanism I learned at home.

However, after identifying the source of my depression, I did what I had learned to do. I didn't tell anyone. I got busy with the psychological task of burying it again so that I could continue ignoring the painful loss.

But there is some digging I have been able to do over time. Excavating the past in order to find answers to basic questions has been difficult work. A simple question like "How did you learn to speak English?" lacked an answer. Through much reflection, I was able to see it was on the grounds of the Sibley Manor complex—its courtyards, side yards, and backyards. That's where I pinpoint the moment, though of course language acquisition is far more complex.

That day I remember, I played with a bunch of Cuban children—boys and girls together. Many of the kids were older, like Luis, who had gone to school in English. Now in second grade, he had more English words in his vocabulary, though his comprehension was minimal.

Sadly, I didn't understand what the others were saying as they incorporated English words into Spanish expressions. I was excluded. The norms of my Cuban community were changing. Though it was a beautiful day, I returned to the apartment and my mother. She told me to go back outside to play, but I resisted. I explained why. She encouraged me to go on.

Obediently, I went. That afternoon, on the grounds of the Sibley Manor apartment complex, the English language began making sense to me. I understood English! I ran back inside the apartment to share the triumph with my mother.

Courtyard vocabulary wasn't sufficient. The kindergarten teacher or my classmates at Homecroft Elementary School didn't have those words. I didn't understand them. Why should I go there? Why spend hours with people I didn't know or understand in that ugly building?

Luis was at St. Therese Catholic School, as was José Beruvides. Later, the school merged with St. Leo's Catholic School and later still with St. Gregory's Catholic School. Today, Highland Catholic School is their consolidation.

José's sister, Ariana, was younger than me by a year and one day, too young to be in my class. I was the only Cuban, the dark one who didn't speak English.

Homecroft Elementary held confusion and pain. I came to understand the Spanish expression that translates, *I haven't lost anything there.*

Let me explain. Since I didn't speak English, I didn't have any friends. My classmates didn't know how to respond to me. Also, my name and my complexion were liabilities. I'm sure the descendants of Northern Europeans found me odd. They must have thought of me as a Native American or African American. Those two peoples were their only points of reference in this northern land. Generally speaking, neither one of those ethnicities, at the time, was held in highest esteem.

This desire to not participate, to not go where others are going, "to not lose anything there," has been with me since then. I've shunned Robert Fulghum's *All I Really Need to Know I Learned in Kindergarten* despite its wild popularity. It's now going on my reading list with the hope it will shed more light on those important years.

I'm an introvert, though I am sociable and a skilled public speaker. While I have made most of my living as a professor, groups of people don't invigorate me. I prefer fewer students and small gatherings, quiet swims, especially in natural surround-ings. I meditate and practice a little yoga. I try to limit social situations requiring too much chit-chat. I have played tennis and hiked with a friend. I've run miles alone. Beaches are for swimming but also for scanning the horizon. A vacation alone is a prize!

The need for silence results from my acute hearing. I am fifty-eight years old. A recent hearing test revealed that I hear better than a twenty-year-old. Consequently, I can't get enough silence to compensate for the daily noise, even though the neighbor-hood is quiet. In fact, one of my dreams is to travel way north, above the Minnesota line, into the middle of Canada. There I imagine renting a cabin for a week or two. With little white noise around me, I will hear the earth's natural sounds. I long to hear them.

Introversion and resistance have served me in many ways. However, since I've had to earn a living, the "not wanting to go" has had to be overcome, conversation after conversation, school after school, year after year, job after job. God's angels, family and friends, have kept me going.

Often, as in the case of my kindergarten days, my angel of a mother understood my predicament. I didn't want to be in a community I was unable to be a part of. I couldn't segregate with Cuban students, since I was the only one in the classroom. Often, she relented. I could stay home with her, like I wanted.

There is a stereotype concerning Latinas and their immediate bonding, that is, our ability to establish community within sec-onds. First, we are not as individualistic as people are in the United States, so the move toward community may be swifter. Some Hispanic cultures are more formal and reserved than others. A person from Bolivia's altiplano may have a different temperament than a Spanish Caribbean islander or a coastal person. Depending on the level of enthusiasm displayed when Latinas meet, outsiders may think they are witnessing tremendous bonding. For example, many, many Hispanics greet one another with a kiss on the cheek and take leave from one another in a similar manner. It's an important gesture that means hello and goodbye, nothing else. Strangers may also receive this greeting. Additionally, the use of Spanish language or not, extended families, religious traditions, class, educational level, country of origin, and U.S. experience—these and other factors may or may not facilitate ease.

Latinas are no different from any other smaller group within a larger culture. For instance, St. Augustine has numerous resettled New Yorkers. When I've seen them gather, laughter and conversation abounds. Past experiences and points of view generated by living in New York City are a pleasure to revisit. The immediate common ground, however, does not guarantee the budding of good friendships. My closest friendships are with men and women who either are naturally culturally diverse or have traveled and lived in various regions of the United States or as outsiders in another country. Stronger bonds exist with those friends who are keen on spiritual development.

Despite my refusals to go to school, my parents made attempts to organize my half-days at Homecroft Elementary. A patrol boy from the school lived in our building. He was responsible for walking me to school. I remember his early-morning knocks on the door to get me, my mother often saying no. The door closed. Then, he'd run up the short staircase and out the building's door.

My mother's gentle voice explained that I had to go to school soon, that it was time. Luis Gustavo went to school and he liked it, she said.

I do have a few memories from those kindergarten days. Students brought rugs to school for regularly scheduled naps. I liked the quiet time. The other activities were more difficult to enjoy: sitting on the floor while being read to by a strange adult in a strange language, stacking blocks in one corner of the room, alone, and finger-painting at the art table in silence.

One time the teacher stood near the classroom door and called my name. It was time for me to work on art. For once, I was busy in another corner of the room, building something with another little girl. We weren't talking but we were involved. I didn't want to stop. It is the only memory I have of engaging with a classmate until the fourth grade.

More than likely, the building blocks had caught my attention. This was unusual because, as my father reports, since a very young age I bored easily with toys. I'd play with them a while, then leave them, much like a cat does when the catnip inside a felt mouse has evaporated.

Across the room, the teacher continued calling me and pointing to the long art table. I waited. I liked the blocks. I didn't want the rare connection with a classmate broken.

"I know you understand what I'm saying," the teacher said.

I obeyed.

I left to sit at the table bearing the shame of resisting authority. I feared my parents would learn of it. Having an adult single you out for misbehaving and calling it out for everyone's attention was to be avoided. In a culture that prizes the collective, a public correction sheds light on the character of the entire family, not just on the individual. A Cuban represents his or her family. Any adult could correct a child, by the way. But causing problems for a teacher was particularly disrespectful.

Still, as an adult, I am ashamed if I am called to task about my behavior by a supervisor, an elder, or a friend. How embarrassing.

I work to avoid drawing attention to myself as a result of lack of compliance.

The Cuban model makes room for individuals and their idiosyncrasies. We are family-oriented people, and we include extended families. Often, we are clannish, which inhibits interacting with and committing to the functioning of a larger community. Unless, of course, one belongs to a faith community.

Some blame Catholicism for the shame involved in being singled out for misbehavior. The daily, private review to identify sin results in acknowledgments of failure. Some voices in popular culture contend that such a regular focus on failings erodes self-esteem. Focus on strengths, they say, or you'll not become a fully realized individual.

The opposite is true.

By understanding themselves as fallible, people learn to live in community. How does that happen? We identify failings and confess them to God. We accept his forgiveness; it is hoped we forgive ourselves. From there, we can begin to extend the same mercy to others.

That's where community happens.

It must've been Halloween when Great-aunt Carmen explained the devil was on the loose that day. What a horrible thing! Scared, I stayed inside the basement apartment at Sibley Manor. At one point during the day I looked up to the living room window and saw the devil run past, but I saw only his feet and tail.

Noris Beruvides (now Baldwin) remembers her family's first Christmas at Sibley Manor in 1962. An enormous snowfall came. Church members made sure the family had a turkey for their Christmas meal. In fact, that holiday season, they received three turkeys as gifts.

No doubt my great-aunt immediately adapted her meat marinade to the turkey. She wouldn't have made it any other way. Every year, she made a tender, flavorful turkey at Thanksgiving, a new holiday for us. The basic ingredients making it come alive for our palates are Spanish: olive oil, fresh garlic, lime, vinegar, salt, and pepper. The bird marinates for several days. Cuban traditional side dishes are served with it. The foods cooked in her Sibley Manor kitchen made us feel we weren't far from our island.

Traditional foods—malanga, plantains, black beans, coffee, cassava, even Spanish nougats—were ordered from a small grocery store in South St. Paul. One crossed the Wabasha Street Bridge over the Mississippi River to get there, my father said.

Somehow, a Cuban resident of Sibley Manor found the store. The proprietor was a Russian who had lived in Cuba. About twelve or fourteen Cuban families in St. Paul would love to place special grocery orders, he said.

The Russian welcomed the Cubans. His bodega-like store was a good place to gather with other exiles, swapping stories while picking up orders. The Russian knew their hanging around and talking was not loitering. Miami Cubans struggled with that interpretation.

The Russian was fluent in Spanish, having moved to Cuba to escape the politics of his native country. When he saw the direction the revolution was taking, he packed and left Cuba, bypassing Miami and heading straight to Minnesota, where he settled. He lamented leaving Cuba almost as much as he did the loss of his own country.

The Russian called people when their orders arrived from a wholesale warehouse in Chicago. Thanks to him, our family and many others did not have to change their diets much while they were undergoing the changes implicit in living in such a different environment.

～

The traditional Cuban Christmas Eve and New Year's Eve meals feature pork; the garlicky pig is slow-cooked for hours in a backyard pit, if one is lucky. Side dishes include black beans and rice or, if you're from the Eastern Provinces, a red beans and rice dish called *congri oriental*. There's a green salad, boiled cassava with *mojo* garlic and oil sauce, plantains, bread, and then desserts. The Spanish *turrones* or nougat candies hit grocery store shelves in Miami sometime in October, when people are starting to consider gifts and guests during the holiday season.

In Cuba, while Christmas Eve remained important, we opened gifts in Cojímar on Christmas Day. At the time, in Havana, some people were adopting this American custom. However, throughout the rest of the island, Three Kings Day remained the traditional day for opening gifts. That's how my parents were raised.

In Minnesota, we kept Christmas Day for gift opening so as to keep in alignment with the larger U.S. culture. Christmas Eve was still important, as was attending Mass on either of the two days.

Generally speaking, there's not much hedging with Cubans. They'll tell you what they think, some more softly than others.

If you're a child and a Cuban adult gets a hold of you to let you know for a final time you're not behaving properly, watch out! A tug of the hair, a pull on the ear, a slap on the hand, a long, hard look for some. A looming threat was of the *tapaboca*—our mouth being slapped if our language or responses toward our elders was disrespectful. A *galleta,* which literally means cracker in English, means a slap, another strike to avoid.

Later, when my siblings and I were older and bolder and settled in another, bigger house, our mother issued warnings for us to control ourselves. When she tired of coaxing, she'd remove a shoe and fling it at one of us across the room. If she missed and we laughed, that was worse. We were, at times, intolerable.

In extreme cases, when we didn't respond to the authority of my mother or grandmother or aunt, my father learned of the matter when he got home from work. He pulled a leather belt out of pant loops and chased us.

"El cinto! El cinturón!" Holy Moses! Not the belt! We ran and screamed and were spanked and cried. For a time, we were better behaved. We were sorry, for a while.

The best part of going to kindergarten when I did go was that my great-uncle Epifanio walked me home. He didn't hold my hand but walked beside me. During the winter, I walked behind him on the narrow cleared path of icy sidewalk, where boot prints made in slush became like fossils when temperatures dropped again.

Great-uncle Epifanio Echevarria was a tall, thin man who smoked cigarettes. He wore a dark-gray wool cardigan with a white button-down shirt underneath it and black pants. That was his uniform. His Adam's apple protruded. His white hair was thick and combed back. He wore black-framed glasses. He spoke some English. He loved baseball and knew many of the Spanish-speaking Twins players. He was a quiet man who loved to read, especially history and politics. Cuban national politics were important. His son Orlando inherited his father's love of reading and of politics. Both men kept their eyes and minds on political developments in the United States and Cuba.

Every Sunday after church we gathered for a big lunch, the day's main meal. Afterward, Epifanio napped in a chair. He snored.

Some Sibley Manor Saturdays my father volunteered to be the community barber for the Cuban boys. He didn't have any training for it. No one had. However, he took on the task because it needed to be done and no one else dared to do it. With a scissors and comb my father made the Cuban boys from Sibley Manor presentable. He saved their parents money.

When the word spread that our family planned to move to Merriam Park after a year, the Cubans found a way to formally thank my father for his services as a barber. They pooled their money and bought a barber's kit with an electric shaver that had different nozzles. That was a beautiful gesture, my father said. For many years, he used the electric shaver on my brothers.

My father and Epifanio visited the Beruvides family on Saturdays. Noris brewed Cuban coffee and my father played Spanish classical guitar.

Roberto Beruvides tried to teach my great-uncle to drive. After each attempt, Roberto returned to the apartment shaking his head, dismayed with his lack of progress.

"I don't know if he'll be able to learn," Roberto said to Noris.

Epifanio Echevarria never drove in Cuba or in the United States. On the island, he lived within a block of his job. So he walked to work, as did most of the people in the small northern coastal town of Punta San Juan, Camaguey, Cuba. When he found work in the Twin Cities he got there by foot, bus, or commuting with my father.

Wherever Epifanio worked, he was good at it. His son Orlando remembered that when his parents first arrived in Minnesota, his father got a factory job assembling boxes. He liked the work, though it was piece work. Two or three months into the job, his employer called, asking him to slow down. The union complained he was too productive.

Eventually, at Twin City Meats, my father's boss asked if he might know of someone, someone who spoke English, to fill a position in the company's seafood department. The job didn't carry a big salary with it, but it was full-time work.

"I know the man," my father said.

Epifanio started at Twin City Meats, riding to work with my father every day.

In Cuba, Epifanio Echevarria had kept the books at a sugar mill called Central Punta Alegre. That's where he met Maria del Carmen Ballesteros. With her father, she and her younger sister Manuela had come to Cuba early in 1923 from Ledesma, Spain. After a year working at the sugar mill, their father returned to his new wife and life in Spain, leaving his daughters on the island.

The Cubans were outraged by his act, which they saw as parental abandonment, though the young women worked and were housed with good families. My great-aunt and grandmother were scared, embarrassed, and devastated by what their father had done. They never spoke about their early days as immigrants to Cuba. Apparently, those memories were too painful.

My great-aunt Carmen did return to Spain to visit her father and stepmother, years later, with her son Orlando. My grandmother Manuela never returned. I don't know why. She was younger than her sister when she came to Cuba and identified more as Cuban. I heard her mourn the loss of Cuba, but never the loss of her native Spain.

Great-aunt Carmen was a beautiful, religious woman as well as a skilled seamstress. In time, her sewing, upholstery work, and knitting skills were recognized for their excellence. Like my grandmother Manuela, she was a top-notch home cook. Eventually, when she married and had children, her earnings helped to educate her sons. Hector died in 1942 in Cienfuegos, Cuba. Orlando became a physician and died in 2015 at age eighty-four in Fort Myers, Florida.

In Cuba, her skills and integrity were noticed by Mr. Jenkins, the general manager of the sugar mill. Mrs. Jenkins also appreciated my aunt's work whenever she visited from the United

States with their two daughters. Beyond new garments, the Jenkins family hired her to make all sorts of domestic things—curtains, pillows, bedspreads. She also did upholstering.

The families maintained a friendship for many years. The Jenkins visited my parents in Cojímar when they came to Havana from the interior. When the revolution came, Jenkins loved Cuba so much that he stayed. At least, that's where he was when we boarded the airplane and came to Florida, my father said.

But those were other times. Punta Alegre, El Central. Life was good there. Only my grandmother Manuela reminded us of our past. When she lived with us in Minnesota, she mourned our previous way of life. My parents hoped she would quiet, like they had.

Meanwhile, my grandmother and her sister talked about El Central. I didn't know where it was. No one unfolded a map to explain. If life was so good there, why weren't we living there? Why did my parents bring us to a place where we lived such a second-class life? My grandfather stayed in Cuba. Why? A long time passed before I understood the answers to these questions.

My great-aunt Carmen bought a sewing machine and was back to work. She made our best clothes. She knit beautiful wool sweaters and dresses. In another era, she would've been an exalted textile artist. She is one of the countless home cooks and seamstresses who should've been called chef and artist with income corresponding to these talents.

Luis Gustavo remembers our first snow, I don't. He said a group of Cuban children were in the courtyard at Sibley Manor, waiting for snow. The day was dark. Finally, big, fluffy flakes flew down. The overly bundled children ran to catch them with their tongues. Luis followed. Our mother saw him, was horrified, and hauled him indoors.

Our mother was slender. Yet that winter she gained weight and girth, as a child was due in February. She didn't buy maternity clothes but adapted her skirts using a diaper pin to close the growing gap. The modification must have been uncomfortable. My mother lived with it since she knew fabric and notions cost money, even if her aunt Carmen could sew a few garments for her.

One of the Lauer girls came to visit that winter with some of her classmates from the nearby Catholic high school. She asked what we needed as time for the delivery approached.

My father, trying to get a chuckle, said, "Maria needs a new zipper!"

The girls were confused. Maybe they didn't understand his accented English. My mother lifted a sweater to illustrate how she kept her skirts wearable. Everyone laughed. The charitable girls raised money to help with the layette for the coming infant.

I remember my mother was absent from the apartment. Where had she gone? My father took my brothers and me to a parking lot outside a large brick building, St. Luke's Hospital, one afternoon to find her. We looked up to see our mother waving from a window in a top floor. She was fine, just staying in another place. She'd be home soon. I didn't know a baby sister would be with her.

One winter day when I didn't go to school, I remember going into my parents' bedroom. The bed was made. A baby was lying on it. My mother closed a diaper pin on each side of a cloth diaper. By the light, it was late afternoon. The apartment was quiet. No one else was home but my mother, the baby, and me. I was content.

The other *americano* born to the Sibley Manor Cubans came more than a year later, in August 1964: Robertico Beruvides. He was named Roberto, but the diminutive distinguished him from his father.

Cuban children call adult family friends by their first names. Noris was not Mrs. Beruvides. Keti was not Mrs. Beguiristain. Their husbands were Roberto and Luis.

Children are taught to use the formal address of *Usted* for adults. If you're an adult, you use it with people you've just met. If that happens to be another Cuban, it won't be long before he or she tells you directly: "Don't use *Usted,* it makes me feel old. Use the *tu.*"

In a way, using the *tu* is the beginning of *confianza.* More relationship time must pass before one receives a person or family's *confianza.* The level of intimacy allows a person a closer look inside a family's dynamics. If *confianza* exists, for instance, I answer the door and invite a guest in, even if the house lacks order. If people have *confianza* between them, they overlook such a slack.

Have you walked into a family argument? No matter, you are *de confianza.* You might be asked an opinion about the issue under discussion. If a child is screaming or slamming doors in disagreement when you arrive, more than likely you will express empathy and acknowledge similar struggles.

Two weeks after Robertico was born, the building's caretaker wanted to see the infant. Noris welcomed the visit, as any young mother would. She didn't speak much English at the time.

The apartment's cleanliness and tidiness astonished the caretaker. Shortly afterward, she recommended the Beruvides couple to share the building caretaker position. They were the first Cuban caretakers in Sibley Manor, opening doors for other

Cubans to obtain similar positions. Rent was reduced. In fact, their work was so good, they won an award for maintaining the cleanest building! The prize was a dinner at Gannon's Restaurant along with cash.

Rare is the Cuban who does not keep a clean house. In Cuba, tiled or terrazzo floors are swept and mopped daily. Mold won't grow under daily showers of vinegar and water. Keeping homes disinfected promotes good health. Besides, it's nice to have fans blowing without dust scattering. It's good to prepare food when, if the boric acid lining your cabinets has to be replaced, roach waste is wiped off counters.

When Luis and I were in Cuba, we played a game that illustrates the cultural focus on cleanliness that we, at young ages, already subscribed to.

Here's how it went: Luis Gustavo indicated someone had spit in a particular spot. Or he said a particular spot was dirty. The possibility of the existence of either state caused such disgust that I vomited. When that happened, he was so repulsed, he'd do the same.

The last time we played this game was in Miami. I remember Luis running in the little rented house, then skidding in my vomit. Great-aunt Carmen had had enough of cleaning floors, washing clothes, and giving baths. She spanked us so much we stopped playing the game.

My younger brother Juan Carlos is absent from my memories of Sibley Manor. He was three years old, being watched by my great-aunt and uncle upstairs, especially after Glenna was born. He was our aunt's favorite. My mother certainly appreciated the help.

Juan Carlos, Luis, and I shared a bedroom with bunk beds and another single bed. We slept across the hall from our parents and the baby. That winter our bedroom window was cracked for ventilation.

Unfortunately, my parents' interest in good air quality became a factor in my catching pneumonia. We were off to the hospital, where I stayed for three days, my mother and father rotating night shifts to be my advocates.

This caused a tug-of-war with the nuns who were nurses there.

"You should go home," they said. "We're nurses."

But my mother came to my defense with logic.

"She doesn't speak English. How will you know what she needs?"

They yielded.

Round-the-clock visitation was not the modus operandi during the early 1960s. Fortunately for patients and their loved ones, U.S. hospitals have liberalized visiting hours. There's a literature on its benefits.

Whenever I pass the open doors of patients on the way to visit someone I know, I am saddened to see anyone without company. Some prefer it. They don't want to impose on others. Or they know people are afraid of being exposed to bacteria.

Despite these objections, hours in a hospital room pass slowly. A television is no solace, especially if it is dueling with a roommate's set.

Some people avoid the sick, especially if they are in hospice care.

Meanwhile, the dying patient wonders what happened to so many of his or her friends. Are they too busy to stop by for ten minutes to say goodbye?

No one likes the accessories to disease. It hurts to see how sick a person can become, how mangled, how pock-marked and feverish. Tubes, plastic pouches, the smells of urine and bowel

movements, the spitting up, the wiping of the mouth, the spoon-
fuls of ice chips hand-fed to those fresh from surgery.

Remembering the person in a hammock, sipping a ginger
beer, is better. She looked nicer then.

Cubans, generally speaking, insist on visiting the sick. They
come to hospital bedsides in numbers, setting up living quarters in the patient's room. Some sleep at the bedside in reclin-
ers. Others stay for hours. If too many are in the room, they
chat with others in a waiting area. In Miami, it is an accepted
practice.

A lack of staff contributed to the creation of this custom.
Today, even with well-staffed hospitals and trained nurses on all
shifts, the custom remains. A visitor adjusts a pillow or feeds
the patient. A family member ensures medications are timely.
The doctor's visit is recognized. Visitors ask questions for the
patient, especially when he or she is drugged or asleep.

In other words, Cubans are not fans of HIPPA. Since the
family is affected by the illness of one member, the family claims
its right to know medical details concerning the one in bed.

During our final days at Sibley Manor, the summer of 1963, our
family was having a picnic with another Cuban family at a park
in St. Paul.

There, on those soft rolling grounds, Margot Romillo, a
Cuban woman in town visiting family, heard Spanish spoken
with a familiar accent. She approached the group.

Friendship with the resettled Beguiristain-Romillo family
began.

Keti Romillo de Beguiristain was twenty-eight years old when
she and her four children arrived in Miami on July 17, 1961. Luis
III was six, Pablo four, Xavier two, and Maribel one. Soon, Keti
welcomed her niece and nephew, Mary and Jose Luis Porto,

who were eight and six. Her husband Luis Beguiristain II arrived in Miami a few months later, in September.

In Miami, Keti found work as a secretary for the Cuban Refugee Program section of Church World Service at the Freedom Tower. Her English skills were excellent, as she had graduated from Greenville College in South Carolina. Luis Beguiristain II had mechanical engineering degrees from the University of Pennsylvania and the University of Havana. In Cuba, he owned and operated two sugar mills.

In those days, the majority of Cubans had some allegiance to the Roman Catholic Church. Those who wanted to resettle registered to do so with Catholic Relief Services. Keti remembers many Protestant churches had willing sponsors—both individual and congregations. They offered to sponsor refugees, even if the candidates were not Protestants. They wanted to help.

Macalester Presbyterian Church helped the Beguiristains resettle in St. Paul on December 15, 1962. Their first home was on Cambridge Avenue in an upper duplex. Immediately, they learned about the Cuban activities of the International Institute of Minnesota. Keti Beguiristain met my mother at a reunion there, but didn't encounter her again until her sister Margo made the serendipitous connection.

So our Cuban community in Minnesota expanded. While blanket statements do not cover exceptions, I can say that once you befriend a Cuban, you will meet many others. Many Cubans welcomed extended family to the Twin Cities, even for short visits.

A robust connection with extended family members is less common for the "prized" nuclear American family. Unfortunately, such insistence on individuality leads to an insurmountable loneliness. Ask a general physician about the percentage of patients seeking treatment for depression in her practice.

I'd be foolish to forsake the social wealth characteristic of Hispanic cultures.

My parents prepared to move from Sibley Manor to a Merriam Park duplex. The neighborhood was close to downtown, so my father had an easy commute. In addition, three blocks away was a Catholic elementary school and church.

Our great-aunt and uncle moved too. Luis Beguiristain II helped my father move them to a nearby apartment.

Our little community continued growing.

Many Minnesotans came alongside, enjoying a chance to use their Spanish language or to acquire more of it. Others liked our strong, sweet coffee. In turn, we started pulling off boots in their foyers and putting stocking feet on their carpets.

We were, in fact, adapting to some of their ways.

Dark-looking people came out of the house on the corner opposite: Greeks, my stepmother said, there's another family of them at the end of the block.

—Samuel Hynes, *The Growing Seasons*:
An American Boyhood Before the War

[CHAPTER 5]

Spanish is the language of my emotional life, the language of my heart, though I am now English dominant. It will be the language of my deathbed, so I hope bilingual staff is available when that happens. I have had the privilege to visit a few bilingual people in their last days. Whether their first language was English or Spanish, the first language becomes prominent as they weaken.

Until the age of ten, when my English language skills were fluent, my memories of the transitions from one dwelling to another are missing, no matter how I try reviving them. Sometimes I think the moves were so troublesome my unconscious mind refuses to release them. Other times I think the inability to remember them is a salute to my parents, who eased the moves so they were seamless. The dwellings I've called home are like landscapes of individual dreams.

Perhaps children, having lived so little, don't find regular changes disruptive. For example, if your family follows the harvest in order to earn a living, then setting up and taking down households is routine. Life is a sequence of new lodgings and schools, other families and friends, hearing a different language and not understanding it comes with new territory. A regular diet of dramatic change early on and a child defines living in those terms. It's the only way he or she has lived.

Likewise, children raised in one place with one language and one ethnic group think that's how everyone experiences life.

Nevertheless, migrant farmworker children, for example, know people from their communities who are settled. In some ways, staying put is advantageous, particularly for children. Otherwise, their education, that valuable commodity, is interrupted when crops are ready in another state.

We weren't migrant farmworkers, although in many states other than Florida people have confused me for one. Suggesting even a slight comparison between the hard lives of migrant farmworkers and ours may be disrespectful to them. In this country, we were initially poor but educated people, middle-class refugees. However, we were displaced people on the move. That pattern, established early in the Veiga children, had assets and liabilities. Both were made clearer as we moved toward young adulthood.

No other families moved as often. The Lauers remained at their house and farm. The Beruvides family kept their Sibley Manor apartment.

From their first apartment, the Beguiristains moved to a rented house in Highland Park. A year later, when the owner put the house on the market, they opted to buy a different house in the same neighborhood. In 1964, they secured enough for a down payment for a house on Hartford Avenue. They lived there until 1977, when they moved to Houston, Texas. Thirteen years in one place—I have yet to accomplish that feat.

Ultimately, I am grateful for a childhood lived without parents dodging the landlord every first or fifteenth of the month. I never feared a knock on a front door delivering an eviction notice. Soldiers didn't come in the middle of the night to take anyone to a prison cell. The green of the fatigues of the militia, it's a color I was forbidden to wear. I avoid it still.

St. Paul's Cuban children were asked to sing Christmas songs as part of the holiday festivities at the International Institute. In fact, my father was president of the Cuban group there for a few years. Children were recruited. Rehearsals began. Keti Beguiristain was an enthusiastic choir director. We gathered in the basement of her house, practicing songs in Spanish. Thanks to her efforts, I can sing *Arbolito* to this day, the only Christmas song I know from beginning to end in Spanish. I cherish it.

Being exiled Cubans in Minnesota was a common bond, but friendships did not thrive on that alone. The Cuban women talked about their families. Their children might fall in love and marry, who knew what the future would bring? In this way, our families would be in-laws, not only friends.

Grandmother, Great-aunt, and Great-uncle were also close to the Beguiristains. Luis III, Pablo, and Xavier especially appreciated my great-uncle Epifanio, who, along with their father or ours, took children to watch the Minnesota Twins play ball.

I accompanied the boys to the ballpark, especially during the summers on Ladies Day, during the middle of the week, when girls and women got in free. Unlike football, I could understand more about how the game was played. The sport was and still is big with Cubans. Some of the players spoke Spanish. A few were Cuban! These were added attractions. When we had lower seats near the outfield and innings changed, we sometimes called to the players in Spanish. Kindly, the ballplayers returned greetings.

Pedro Ramos, born in Pinar del Río, Cuba, had left the Twins by 1961, a year before we arrived in town. Pitcher Camilo Pascual was Havana-born.

Tony Oliva, also from Pinar del Río, joined the Twins in 1962, the year we got to town. He stayed in Minnesota with his family. The right fielder was a designated hitter, one of six players initially inducted into the team's Hall of Fame.

My brother Juan Carlos was a huge Oliva fan. He imitated Oliva's swing when he played baseball at home or at school.

Zoilo Versalles also played for the Twins at the time, as shortstop. Born in the Vedado neighborhood of Havana, Cuba, Versalles died in Bloomington, Minnesota, at fifty-five. According to Wikipedia, he was "eternally homesick for his native Cuba."

Later, in 1967, Rod Carew, who was born in Gatun in the Panama Canal Zone, joined the Twins, playing first and second base. He, too, was generous enough to return a few words of Spanish in reply to our calls.

The ball games provided experiences where I felt special, not oddball outcast special, but neon light special. The Cuban kids spoke Spanish to famous ballplayers from the stands! The American kids couldn't do that. For once, we were cool.

That September, we moved to a big white house at 1835 Dayton Avenue. I was five, turning six in November.

The rented duplex in Merriam Park doubled our living space. In my view, it was not a good place to live as it was too big to feel safe. The square footage translated as scary. My fears were confirmed. The attic and basement proved to be frightening.

Family members couldn't see one another all the time in the duplex. The place was too big. I felt safer in the little rentals in Miami as well as our two basement dwellings. In those homes, unless you shut the bathroom door, there wasn't a time when you didn't see or weren't able to be seen by someone.

Secondly, the house was old. We had never lived in such an old place. In 1963, it was old but not ready for the demolition ball. Built in 1906, the house was designed by a well-known architect, Louis F. Lockwood, born in England, an immigrant to St. Paul in 1892. During his years in Minnesota, Lockwood designed about seventy structures. Twenty to twenty-five of them are in the Summit Avenue area. One year after this house was completed, in 1907, Lockwood died.

As a result of its design and craftsmanship, the house continued past its centennial and increased in value. In 2014, according to the property assessment by Ramsey County, it was worth $338,100.

Another unsettling trait was that the house—which looked like a four-square single-family unit—was partitioned inside. A wall sliced it in two from the top of its roof to the basement. The undivided structure is 3,527 square feet, so our quarters were half that number. The McNally family, with two children, lived on the other side of the great wall. Bright red hair distinguished Colleen, the oldest child. Her brother Jerry was about Luis Gustavo's age.

Jerry McNally kept a ten-gallon aquarium that was home to tropical plants, fish, and snails. Luis was intrigued by the snails and asked if Jerry could give him one, as my birthday was coming. When the day came, I wasn't too keen on the snail, Luis noticed, so he was obliged to care for it. My brother's lifelong hobby was born. Eventually, our mother bought him a copy of *Dr. Innes' Exotic Aquarium Fishes* so he would learn the science of fish-keeping.

It was time to start anew. Always, it was time to start anew. I don't recall being given explanations, though my parents might have offered them. The elders made decisions. The children would abide by their decrees without much fuss. Signs of resistance created trouble. Options weren't presented. Once, my mother herded us into the station wagon for a Sunday visit to a couple without children. We dreaded the hours of adult conversation without new playmates or toys.

"You're going, and you're going to have fun!" she said, closing a door on the station wagon.

Luis Gustavo and I started the 1963–64 school year at St. Mark's Catholic School. He started third grade while I began first. My classroom was 102, on the left when you walked into the school building from the Dayton Avenue entrance. Luis had left St. Therese's and his classmates there, including a few other Cuban boys.

St. Mark's Catholic School—like it or not, that's where we were going. Staying home was not a choice; I couldn't negotiate it. Home is the best place to be. My great-aunt Carmen repeated that sentence like a mantra.

"Where else can you go?" she'd ask after saying it.

I've met and talked with children poised to start first grade, an "official" entry into school. For the most part, they are excited about the prospect. They can't wait to meet their new teacher and find new friends among their classmates. Going to school is a new world they anticipate.

In contrast, my familiar friend at school was called dread.

The Sisters of St. Joseph were classroom teachers at St. Mark's who taught alongside lay teachers. The school had opened fifty years earlier, in September 1913.

Good teachers and guardians—the sisters warned us to be careful walking to and from school. Do not accept candy from a stranger, they said. The stranger might even be in a car offering us a ride home.

After that warning, the group of children who walked home together was on the lookout for such a person. No doubt he was a hobo, dirty. Homeless men were called hobos then. We only knew about the men. Today, we know the homeless population includes women and children and people of all ages and backgrounds.

One weekend afternoon when Juan Carlos and I were playing on the sidewalk, we saw such a man. He stood in filthy clothes without speaking. A puddle was beneath him as if he'd urinated there. Terrified, we ran home.

The neighborhood burst with children. A few years earlier, during the 1960–61 academic year, St. Mark's enrollment peaked with 1,534 children.

Today, enrollment is about three hundred students. The school's website boasts a culturally diverse student body. Furthermore, the school's curriculum for students—preschool to eighth grade—includes required Spanish language classes. My great-aunt Carmen would've been pleased with the inclusion of Spanish language as part of the curriculum. I see her nodding her head in agreement. The *americanos* had finally caught on.

Great-aunt Carmen Echevarria was right. She was ahead of her time. In spite of our resistance I appreciate her insistence on our keeping our native language. She did us a huge favor.

"Hablen Castellano! Hablen Castellano!" Those words belong to my great-aunt, demanding we speak in Spanish. If she hadn't insisted, she wouldn't have been able to communicate with us. Her grandchildren in Illinois spoke only English, at least during their childhood.

Spanish remained alive, however halted, in Minnesota. Meanwhile, English words multiplied like spores.

At St. Mark's, I remember the desks, the black chalkboard, and one of the sisters at the front of the classroom. At the school day's end, felt erasers were slapped together to release the chalk. Boards were wiped with big sponges. But I remember little else, probably because I didn't know what was being said. Memory is linked to language; as a result, I remember scenes from my youngest days in Cuba, but few about my early school days in St. Paul. This is how I explain the lapses to myself.

I remember a little girl who lived across the street. Sarah lived in a big old house too. More than likely, we met walking home from school on elm-lined Dayton Avenue. She invited me over to play. I don't recall her coming to our house. I visited only a few times. The visits petered when winter came.

My grandmother Manuela lived with us then. She'd come from her son Homero's house in Valencia, Venezuela, to help when Glenna was born. Among her many contributions to the smooth running of the household, she babysat when my mother ran errands.

Once, our dentist called the house for assistance—his patient spoke only Spanish. The patient turned out to be the Twins player Tony Oliva! And my mother, who had been his translator, invited him home for coffee. He came while we were in school so we missed seeing the important visitor.

In our bedroom, while she sat in a chair hand-stitching, my grandmother told me that my friend Sara's mother was dead. A mother died. It was a terrible thought. How did it happen?

"Sara's mother had been sewing," my grandmother said, putting a needle into a tomato-shaped pin cushion. "The sewing needle went into her body. Sewing needles don't have heads, like pins have, so the doctor couldn't grasp it and pull it out."

What a horrible thing, I thought. She continued.

"The needle floated to her heart and pierced it. That caused her to die. We have to be very careful with sewing needles," she said.

The Dayton Avenue house was spooky because of its dark wood, creaky floors, and places where monsters could hide. It was where I learned bad things could happen beyond its doors.

Otherwise, the house was inviting. A few steps up to the squat house's front door led to an enclosed front porch shared by both units. Our front door was a second front door. It opened to a living room with a fireplace, a dining room, and in the back, a kitchen. A kitchen door led to the backyard. Another kitchen door led to the basement. A basement door led to concrete stairs up into the backyard.

After climbing a long staircase to the second floor, you took a few steps into a large bathroom. The tub was huge and wonderful, like a private pool. Just as they wash their floors daily, Cubans avidly shower. During the summer months in Miami, I often showered three times a day. Showering twice a day is normal for a Cuban. It is common to hear Cubans mention their showering habits. We prod people who are not so inclined into the shower, exasperated by their lack of desire to be clean.

As a result, our skin took a beating during the winter. Our doctor said we shouldn't bathe daily—the climate was drier than in the subtropics. The indoor heating elements contributed to lack of humidity. The elders were horrified.

On the left-hand side of the second-floor hallway as you walked to the front of the house was my parents' room, followed by my brothers' room, then the bigger front room. There, my sister and I shared a room with our grandmother.

I hadn't seen her since Cuba—why not? Where had she gone? Here she was again, our stout grandmother, with hazel eyes and long dark lashes. She wore beautiful, dangling earrings. She was affable. She liked to laugh; she employed irony.

An old chair was in the corner of the room. That's where my grandmother rocked my sister to sleep, despite my parents' plea to not set that pattern. She refused to adopt another method.

My parents were keen on establishing a system that worked for American families with many children. The Lauers advised giving the baby a bottle with a little toy attached to it when it was time to go to sleep. Glenna would learn to comfort herself. In that way, my mother could attend to other matters, including putting three other children to sleep. Every night until she died, my mother sat on our bedsides to pray with us.

My grandmother sat in the chair and rocked and sang to Glenna, claiming her right to do so because she was the grandmother. She pulled the "I am your elder" card on my parents. Because of their upbringing, they didn't argue any further with her. She was maladapted for the new lifestyle but proper for the former one.

She was the elder. The old-world ways worked. She rocked and sang to my sister until the old chair collapsed into pieces.

My mother knew her mother would return to Venezuela. Re-establishing a bedtime pattern for the baby would be an ordeal.

Meanwhile, I was glad my grandmother shared our room, especially after one nightmare that came before the chair's demise.

I saw a dark figure with a marquise-shaped head sitting in the chair. Then, it started to rise from it. I was terrified.

I screamed. My grandmother's figure appeared in the doorway, the hall light behind her. She assured me nothing was there. To this day, I can see the creature's thin, human-like body. It personified death. My grandmother dispelled the spirit that was coming toward me.

This bedroom was also where, without permission, I took my eight-month-old sister out of the crib and dropped her. I was afraid I had damaged her forever, but this wasn't the case. I never took her out of the crib again.

It was where I learned President John F. Kennedy had been shot and killed in Dallas, Texas. I was playing with paper dolls on the bed. It was a Friday, November 22, 1963. I don't know if the school had sent us home after telling students the news, but the bedroom was where I recall learning about it.

Other news that day was that a new cousin, Lisa, was born to Orlando and Carol Echevarria, far away in a place called Illinois.

I listened to news of birth and death and continued playing with my dolls. Perhaps I had no visible reaction because, already, news of political upheaval was part of how life was lived. Death could happen. And then, new life could come along.

It is good to learn these realities at a young age, however frightening.

I was quiet, probably hoping, like most children who live with chaos, that if I behaved, the world would as well. Terrible possibilities ran through the world. A mother could die, a needle racing to her heart. No one could stop it. No one could stop a president from being killed, either. The basement and attic doors could be shut. Yet the monster of death could, like a ghost, come through those doors. In fact, it might slip past our front door.

And one day a decade later, without a knock, it did. My beautiful mother died of cancer. She was forty-six and I was sixteen.

Our Miami-based paternal grandparents came to visit for a month while we were at Dayton Avenue. Miguel and Evangelina Veiga were glad for the respite. In Miami, the Cuban exile population reeled with sorrow and uncertainty. Cubans mourned their losses. They waited for news of their loved ones on the island. They worked low-paying jobs and tried to land more of the same. Miami became an anxious city bursting with grateful but grieving refugees.

This Dayton Avenue house was where my great-aunt reupholstered a used sofa, making it flowery and beautiful. My brothers and I took turns sitting on that sofa, especially during the winter, when playing outdoors was limited. We played too hard, too rough, someone might get hurt. Time out on the sofa.

The dining room with lots of cabinets and glass doors was behind the sofa. Dark wood. On the dining room table, Great-aunt Carmen taught us to read in Spanish, after school. She turned the pages of a book and read in Spanish, then I had to do the same. Luis Gustavo had to read too. It was hard to come home from a day of school and have to continue studies beyond homework. No one else did that. The Americans just did homework. Why were we forced to do more?

As a result of the extra effort, Spanish lessons began to be associated with drudgery. So what? The household wasn't democratic. We did what the elders instructed.

Juan Carlos hadn't started reading, though he had begun speaking. Glenna took her first steps in the Dayton Avenue house. Luis Gustavo learned to play chess from neighbor Danny McGillis, who was a year ahead of him in school. By the fourth grade, Luis could beat our father and great-uncle in chess. The game was and is popular with Cubans on both sides of the Florida Straits.

Our great-aunt Carmen helped my mother when the newspaper photographer came. Prior to the photographer's arrival, my mother had been interviewed for an article by Georgann Koelln, a staff writer for the *St. Paul Dispatch*. She needed a family photo.

Without lipstick, our lips wouldn't be seen in the black-and-white photo. A struggle ensued—I didn't want it on. Not for a photo. Not for anything. I ran away. My great-aunt caught me and put it on.

The article appeared on January 14, 1964. The headline reads, "Grateful Cuban Mother Gladly Helps Fund Drive." My mother, described as an attractive brunette, had volunteered to go knocking on doors to collect money for the March of Dimes. At the time, the article noted, she attended English classes twice a week. A trained pharmacist and optometrist in Cuba, my mother hoped to one day apply for a U.S. license to practice either of her professions. Meanwhile, she had four children to raise.

One day, my father felt a bump near my mother's throat. He was concerned about it, but my mother dismissed it, thinking it was a vertebra on a bone. He encouraged her to see a doctor. The surgeon ascertained it was a sebaceous cyst, benign. Its removal was recommended, since it would grow in a highly visible spot and become uncomfortable and unattractive.

She went to the Mayo Clinic in Rochester, Minnesota, for surgery. My parents disappeared. Our grandmother cared for us. The only other time my mother had been absent she returned with a baby. This time, no one took us anywhere to see her.

My parents returned. A scar trailed across my mother's throat, as if someone had cut it with a scissors. There was no baby.

My mother must've been concerned about my lack of friends. I don't remember having any, other than the few visits with Sarah. The company of my brothers and their friends was good enough. In the spring, my mother explained that another mother was a troop leader for the Bluebirds. They met at her house. Her daughter belonged to the group. The woman extended an invitation. I was forced to go. My mother and I walked to the house. She left me.

Many girls were there, both in and out of Bluebird uniform. They were doing a craft project that involved a paper tube from the inside of a roll of toilet paper and a square rubber furniture-caster cup. Glued together, they made a pencil cup. I left with it in one hand, my mother's hand in the other.

I did not join the Bluebirds.

I was happy at home with my family or visiting another family, Cuban or the Lauers, or playing with my siblings and neighbor kids.

Indoors, I coddled a dark-haired Thumbelina doll with a knob on her belly. I wound it for music. My two-story metal dollhouse was satisfying as occasionally I'd get a new piece of furniture for it. I had a Tammy doll instead of the more popular Barbie. She was a girl-next-door type when compared to the big breasted, small-waisted Barbie. Paper dolls were great because of the versatility of their outfits. The dolls had all kinds of adventures.

In time, our parents agreed we could keep two small turtles. I don't know who lobbied for them. The older children had the responsibility of changing the water in the pond and feeding them.

The turtles lived in a clear plastic container shaped like a pond. An island rose in its middle; there, a plastic palm tree was decoration for the green little turtles. Eventually, the creatures got out of the pond. How? Someone stepped on one accidentally. I was on the front porch playing when my mother found it crushed in the living room.

What was the turtle doing there? Who took it out? Who killed it? Oh no! The other one disappeared, but I don't know if its carcass was ever found. My mother more than likely found it after cleaning the house and deposited it in the garbage can. There was no further talk about turtles.

My first year at St. Mark's is a blur. My most vivid memory is from Mary's month, May. The school honored the Blessed

Mother with songs and flowers and a crown. The student body came to the courtyard where recess was held. A statue of Mary was prominently placed there. I learned to sing the following song to the mother of Jesus:

Hail Holy Queen enthroned above, O Maria! Hail Mother of mercy and of love! O Maria! Triumph all ye cherubim, Sing with us ye seraphim! Heaven and Earth resound the hymn. Salve, Salve, Salve, Regina!

∽

May was a happy month—the snow was gone, flowers were blooming. Soon, very soon, I'd be freed from the misunderstandings and restraints of school. I would be outdoors, running and swimming without a schedule.

Summer meant lakeside picnics, often with other Cuban families. While the children were in the water, the adults set food and supplies on tables and opened lawn chairs. Someone lit the charcoal in the grill. My great-aunt pulled long-marinated meat from a container in the cooler. The chicken, pork, or beef was marinated in garlic, salt and pepper, and a little olive oil and lime for the best flavor. When the meat was done, an adult came to the lakeshore to call us out of the water.

We ignored whoever called. Another adult then would appear on the shore hugging beach towels. This time the call was to be heeded.

Wrapped in the warmth of beach towels, we sat at the picnic tables for a good lunch.

A major downside was that after we'd eaten, my great-aunt ruled we had to wait two hours before swimming again. Digestion took two hours. We couldn't risk developing cramps and drowning. My parents agreed with the edict.

Two hours was a lifetime. The American kids didn't wait. They ate, jumped back in the water, and didn't drown. The adults didn't care about what the American kids did. We weren't doing what they did. Two hours. The restriction never lifted.

Summer remains my favorite season, no matter where I've lived, no matter how hot it gets. The season offers so much of what I relish—freedom from the usual obligations, no matter what they are. People are more inclined to outdoor get-togethers, dinners with family and friends. Community increases. The days are longer. Time slows. The water warms for swimming.

The Veigas took regular summer vacations. My parents packed the station wagon and we drove around the state—they wanted to get to know the Minnesota beyond the cities. Often, our great-uncle and aunt came along. We made it to International Falls. We went to Lake Superior, where my great-aunt found a rock, one that fit well in her hand. It was heavy and smooth. She took it to the kitchen, where it became a tool used to mash garlic cloves and tenderize meat. To this day, my siblings and I keep and use a rock in the kitchen, another one of our aunt's many legacies.

Sometimes Minnesota summer nights are chilly. The rented cabins stored wool blankets in the closets. We fished from wooden docks or from rowboats launched from them. Geese squawked and loons called.

Our father taught us fishing basics. From the quiet shore or dock, we easily launched a wooden rowboat. He'd row us out to a spot. We wore life jackets though we could swim. Once, when the worms we'd dug out of the soil were gone, I put a leaf on a hook as bait and lowered the line. Soon, a sunfish wiggled there. What a great place! I thought. I caught a fish with a leaf!

I hoped summer would last forever. I still do.

Another unforgettable place was home to a larger-than-life folk hero, Paul Bunyan, lumberjack of the century. I thought

the giant was alive! Consequently, I wouldn't get close to him.
Fortunately, there were other areas for children where they
might feed hens and chicks, pet rabbits, or marvel at seeing a
fawn.

In public, though my complexion was an anomaly, I was a
regular Minnesota Catholic schoolgirl. I could ice skate and ride
a bicycle. I picked and ate blueberries and sour crab apples. I
planted seeds for morning glories along the backyard fence in
the spring. I swam, sledded, and skated.

But if you looked closely, you'd begin to see the marks of an
outsider. For one, I played outdoors with other children only as
long as my brothers were with me. Unlike my classmates' ear-
lobes, mine were pierced. They were pierced in a Cuban clinic
when I was three days old. I wore an eighteen-karat gold chain
with a holy medal. Though I wore a school uniform, my other
clothes were mostly dresses made by my talented great-aunt.
Luis Gustavo and I didn't sign up for swimming classes at the
local recreation center. We'd learned to swim in Cuba.

Unlike other Minnesotans in the city, my grandmother, aunt,
and uncle were never far away. We didn't get in the car and drive
for an hour or two to visit them. Every day we ate Cuban food,
the black beans pureed. We spoke Spanish. My parents spoke
English with an accent.

First grade ended; somehow, I passed to second. But soon
after classes ended, tragedy struck. A classmate was killed by a
car while crossing the street on June 24, 1964. According to her
neighbor Sheila Sparks, the girl dropped something while crossing Cleveland Avenue. She ran back for it; the car struck her.

I see myself outside St. Mark's Catholic Church, where her
funeral Mass was being held. My mother and aunt are with me.

"Do you remember her? She was your friend," they said.

I didn't say anything.

For years I have replayed the scene, trying to see who she was. She had been a friend, my mother said. Who? Who was my friend back then? No one was my friend at school. No one I remember.

I was terrified. Death came for children too!

I remember the small casket coming up the main aisle of the church. There, the memory ends.

Recently, while I was working in Red Wing, Minnesota, two St. Mark's alumni responded to a Facebook request by Jana Hayden-Sofio, the school's alumni coordinator. Ann Daly and Jim Doelle remembered the little girl's name. Mary Claire Prentice was killed crossing Cleveland Avenue.

When I read her name on the computer screen, my heart sank. I copied it onto a slip of paper. Then I called Jana Hayden-Sofio, to thank her. After a brief conversation, I hung up the phone and sat in the study.

With this name on a piece of paper, her death became more than a memory. I mourned my classmate's death with an adult's sorrow, not a child's terror. I know how much living Mary Claire missed having been killed at such a young age. I am so sorry for her and her family. I am glad to know her name.

The following school year I would be a second grader. I walked more confidently now. I had lost and regained front teeth, permanent adult ones.

The start of the school year began with an embarrassing situation. When it was time to take the school pictures, I missed the chance to wear regular clothing. It was one of the few times when students did not have to wear a uniform. The rarity of the event made it a big deal. Somehow, my parents missed it. In Cuba, school photos were in uniforms. In Minnesota, this was a change and a treat, but somehow, neither of my parents was aware of it.

I managed to button my red cardigan at the top, so in the photograph it looks like I am not wearing a uniform underneath. The photographer may have suggested it. I am smirking in the picture. Ashamed and embarrassed, I wore the costume of a bigger outcast all day long. Only an idiot would wear a uniform to school on a day she didn't have to wear one.

Public shame came again.

In addition, second grade meant I would prepare to receive the next two sacraments, First Confession and Holy Communion. The Second Vatican Council had begun its historic meeting on October 11, 1962, about the time we had settled in Sibley Manor. Officially, the meeting closed on December 8, 1965. Changes came to the altar and to the Catholic community as a result of that meeting. However, those changes hadn't been made at St. Mark's yet. My First Confession and First Holy Communion were in May 1965, a few months before the Vatican Council concluded.

Naturally, Great-aunt Carmen made my outfit, a short-sleeve white cotton faille dress, to the knee, with a Peter Pan collar. The faintly ribbed pattern on the fabric made it drape well; faille was a popular choice for gowns and dresses during the 1940s and '50s. A row of fagoting started from underneath each collar lapel. The open work decoration involved crisscrossing thread across an open seam. The two rows run down the front of the dress toward the hemline, stopping four inches above it.

At a print shop, my parents selected a commemorative card, holy-card size, to announce the important occasion. It is written in Spanish in a font that looks like Old English text; it reads,

"Recuerdo de la Primera Comunion de la niña Marisella Veiga González efectuada en la Iglesia Saint Mark, el día 3 de Mayo de 1965, St. Paul, Minnesota, U.S."

During a classroom practice for Holy Communion, the teacher held a bundle of unconsecrated hosts. She gave us instruction, specifically saying that once the host was in our mouths, we must not touch it. I don't recall instruction on how to dislodge it when it stuck to the roof of my mouth. So my fingers went inside my mouth to bring it down. She corrected me in front of the class.

I was wrong. I was singled out in front of the class. Humiliation again.

We moved closer to the big day.

The day approached. My First Holy Communion dress was in its final stages of construction. Like couture seamstresses, my great-aunt hand-basted every garment for a first fitting. I'd put it on. She'd look at it on my body from a distance, then begin to tug at the shoulder seam or neckline. Sometimes, though it was rare, she declared it fit well. She'd machine sew it then.

After that, I'd return to her apartment for another fitting. I'd get on a wooden box so she could pin the hem line evenly. She'd get on the floor with a dress-hem sewing ruler.

"Turn," she said, putting a straight pin in the fabric. "Turn. Stand up straight."

Hems were hand-sewn. Such trouble! I wanted dresses off the department store rack so I wouldn't have to try them on.

Right before our First Holy Communion, so we wouldn't have time to commit any more sins before receiving it, we had our First Confession. I experienced some anxiety concerning the naming of sins and tracking their frequency. If you said you had committed that particular sin four times, and it was really more like five or six, you had just committed another sin: lying. How was I supposed to remember this?

The sins relevant at the time included disobeying my parents, which I rarely did for fear of reprisal. Saying bad words I suppose, or being angry with one of my brothers.

Early religious training is important so children, parents, and spiritual directors can see behavioral patterns developing. Preparing to receive the sacrament is a valuable part of this. We take the time to reflect on our behavior. How have we failed to love others and, therefore, failed to love God? Countless times. How can anyone put a number on them?

On the day of my First Confession, I remember sitting on a pew in the dark church, eyeballing the confessional. Then, it was my turn. Inside, I knelt and said what I was taught. I asked for the priest's blessing and announced it was my first confession. I listed a few sins, came out, and knelt to complete my penance. Relief came.

I was ready for the next step.

During those days, before the Vatican II announced its changes in the liturgy, Roman Catholics fasted on Sunday mornings until Communion. The American Catholics typically went to brunch after Mass. We didn't go to restaurants. At home or at our great-aunt and uncle's, our family gathered for a big hot lunch.

I felt important having to fast the morning of my First Holy Communion. It signaled something different was about to take place. My classmates and I lined up outside the church, the girls in white dresses and veils. Mine had a crown and waist-long tulle.

I knelt at the communion rail and received the Eucharist.

After Mass, my parents held a party at the house. A photograph was taken with my little sister. There was food and cake. In addition, I got a brand-new green bicycle to ride. It was a great day, like having a second birthday that year but more important.

So I learned to ride a bicycle. I learned fast, no training wheels, my father providing support until I rode alone. Alas, the brakes! In the excitement of riding without support, I'd forgotten to pedal backward for them. I was flying fast on a sidewalk and didn't turn right onto the adjoining sidewalk at the block's end. I crashed into an elm tree. That hurt!

Summer's freedom came in June. I didn't know it then but I should've been saying "so long" to the hallways of St. Mark's. I said goodbye to the McNally family and the backyard and the alleyway where I spent many hours. We weren't consulted or warned about the next move. The move draws another blank.

Our parents bought a house in Roseville. By then, my father was comptroller at Twin City Meats. In September 1965, I would be in third grade at St. Rose of Lima Catholic School. Luis Gustavo would be going into the fifth grade and Juan Carlos would start first grade. The closing on the house didn't coincide exactly with the start of the academic year. We'd be latecomers again.

This move, I suppose, was commendable. Within five years of having left Cuba, my parents had bought their first house in the United States. But at the time, that fact meant little to me. In my world, I'd be starting anew at a third school. I'd be an outsider once more. In addition, I hadn't seen the new house. It might have problems, like the duplex had.

Fortunately, my great-aunt and uncle were moving to an apartment nearby. They were a constant, like our family's faith in God.

When it came to classrooms and classmates, trouble was certain. When they were present, they magnified my status as an alien.

A good host is not only able to receive his guests with honor and offer them all the care they need but also to let them go when their time to leave has come.

—Henri J. M. Nouwen, *Reaching Out:*
The Three Movements of the Spiritual Life

[CHAPTER 6]

Our next home was set between institutions representing two opposite worlds, the spiritual realm and the material one. The brown house with a young paper birch tree in the front yard was at 1404 West Belmont Lane, in the middle of a block-long street. Hamline Avenue intersected the top of the street. Our next Catholic elementary school waited for us there. St. Rose of Lima Catholic School was run by the Servants of Mary. The relatively new Har Mar Mall was at the foot of Belmont Lane. This 1964 move to a ranch-style house signaled another improvement in our family's fortunes. My parents bought it from the Lynch family, who had moved beyond the Roseville suburb to a house on a lake.

The academic year began before the closing on the house took place. We started classes a week or two late. We got the dreaded attention for doing so—once again, notably different, different and late for school.

Mimi Keller (now Pink) was a second grader at the time. Before we moved onto the street, she remembers her mother saying a Cuban family had bought the Lynches' place. There was a possibility for making a new friend, she told her youngest daughter.

Some Belmont Lane homeowners, however, murmured about darkness and differences and awaited to see what we looked like. The Rempel family was odd enough for this suburban, very Catholic street. Mr. Rempel was an older man with a peg leg who raised pigeons and grew flowers smack in the middle of his front lawn. He did not believe in God.

Mr. Rempel gave me my first paying job, picking weeds, the summer before I started fourth grade. He handed me a wooden yardstick to measure how much lawn I had surveyed and cleared of weeds. I was paid five cents a yardstick. The job didn't last long.

His daughter Bonnie was a few years older than Mimi and had befriended her. She took Mimi to get a library card. Mimi liked to visit Bonnie during the late afternoons after she'd finished homework.

Mimi Keller, born to parents of German and Norwegian heritage, had curly brown hair. Her complexion was a shade darker than what is expected among descendants of Northern Europeans and Scandinavians. Minnesota born and bred by Minnesota-born parents, Mimi experienced a childhood stung by cruelty. Some neighborhood children magnified skin color differences, a result, no doubt, of their parents' fears. Mimi was called ugly names and marginalized in her native land.

So when Marilyn Keller suggested her daughter invite me to their house to play, she eagerly came to our door. Having overheard rumors we had darker skin, she figured the attempt was safe. She hoped for a friendship as welcoming as the one she had with Bonnie Rempel.

I inherited my mother's complexion. No one else in the family is darker than my shade of olive brown. I look Mediterranean or

Arabic. My mother inherited her father Severiano González's coloring; his parents were from the Canary Islands, a Spanish territory off Africa's northwest coast. Her mother, my grandmother Manuela, was born in Ledesma, Spain, a small town outside of Salamanca. She was fair with hazel eyes decorated with long, dark lashes. My mother was considered a brunette—brown hair and eyes.

Though his hair was jet black, my father's complexion is fair. When about to go for a swim or to take a shower, he would remove shoes and socks and show his children his smooth, bright white feet and ankles. We rarely saw his feet and toes, and his doing so sent us laughing.

My father's eyes are hazel, as are my siblings' eyes. They have his fair complexion too. Juan Carlos was a celebrated blond-haired child.

Once, in Minnesota, a family friend raved about the beauty of mulatto children. The word *mulatto* is not used now in English, as the words *biracial* or *mixed-race* are preferred adjectives. It is still used in Spanish, however. My mother agreed with her. She had known and seen many mulatto beauties in Cuba. However, she was surprised when she realized the woman referred to me. She explained I was not biracial.

At times, then, I was seen as an Afro-Cuban. Not too many people with that racial and ethnic mix lived in the Twin Cities during the 1960s, with the exception of the Minnesota Twins ballplayer Tony Oliva.

In North Florida, where I now live, I have less explaining to do about my origins, unless I am having a conversation with a snowbird.

I tire of relieving people of their curiosity. If it's our first meeting, they may start visually sniffing around, trying to discern my ethnicity. How is it I speak American English?

Recently, I overheard an Asian American woman, Chicago born and bred, discussing her experience with the same phenomena.

"Where are you from?"

"Chicago."

"No, where are you really from?"

The scenario shows how people want to know her heritage and possibly her allegiance. This dynamic contributes to one feeling like a perpetual outsider, even though one is U.S. born, a child of immigrants. It slows assimilation.

People will see me as they will. Their database may have some information or may require more. Education is needed. Time passes. More than fifty years in this country and I regularly relive discussions about my origins, race, and allegiance, especially when I have lived outside Florida.

Meeting new people is not a joy if you have to discuss a trauma like the loss of your homeland every time you are out for a little fun.

For example, my husband and I declined to attend a Christmas party at a friend's house in December 2014. The party was the weekend after President Obama announced the change in diplomatic relations with Cuba. The nation buzzed with the news, and our little town was not exempt.

"Just tell people you don't want to talk about Cuba, you're at a party," the hostess said when I called with our RSVPs.

"I can't spend the night batting people off. They're curious, I don't want to talk about it, and I don't want to tell them that," I said.

It's my job to educate people sitting in my college classroom, when I am teaching a class. It is not my job to educate anyone over a drink at a social event, where I am enjoying a change of pace with the hope of relaxation.

Wouldn't discussing a trauma that impacted your entire family casually at a party put a damper on your desire to go? How would professional networking be affected?

Discussions surrounding how much "darkness" a person has in one's bloodline are ancient. A former classmate, a Haitian woman who had flown from Italy to take a course in Caribbean fiction writing at the University of Miami, told the class that in Haiti, there are 116 words to describe one's color.

I embrace African contributions to Cuban and U.S. culture. Often, I have wished I were darker, like jet.

Eventually on Belmont Lane, I was dubbed with a nickname that reflected racial perceptions. I was nicknamed Mudd and liked it. Certainly, it was easier to pronounce than Marisella. I was different. At least I was noticed enough to have a nickname, which suggested some kind of affection. Mary Pat Wussler, my friend Janet's mother, did not like to call me Mudd and said so, more than once. She also advocated Mimi use her given name, Marianne.

Juan Carlos's nickname was bestowed by our brother Luis Gustavo, who became Lou. He's kept the name. Since Minnesotans had problems saying "Juan," Luis suggested Young was easier. The nickname had a Chinese ring to it as well as announcing he was younger. The nickname stuck until adulthood. After Juan Carlos married, he asked people to call him JC or Juan. John is his professional name.

Mudd evaporated. Still, whenever I have to give my name for a restaurant waiting list, I sigh.

"Call me M."

I won't make more of a quotidian transaction.

Whenever it's time to meet new people, more specifically non-Hispanics, I know I'm in for an exchange about my country of origin. Often, a challenge arises, "Were you born there or born here?"

Others are dismissive. Without any other information about the lengthy and complex process of assimilation, they announce, "You're All-American! You've been here more than fifty years!"

Bolder folks launch into talking about Cuba. They can't wait to travel there as the forbidden fruit comes closer to their hand.

For me, Cuba and exile are not discussed in two sound bites. Twitter or text, keep it short. That's a demand of popular culture. If you're really interested, I want to say, make a date with me. Before meeting, I'll give you a reading list. When you're done with it, we can discuss the subject for hours. Cuba is worth that investment of time and more.

On December 17, 2014, President Obama made a surprising, controversial announcement smack in the middle of the day: the start of our nation normalizing relations with Cuba. The office of the press secretary at the White House released the text of his statement. In it, President Obama acknowledges some of the history since the 1959 revolution. Cuban exiles and Cubans on the island have "bound America and Cuba in a unique relationship, at once family and foe." It's an appropriate description. Ambiguity is innate to my bicultural experience.

Obama noted that His Holiness Pope Francis appealed to him and to Cuban leader Raul Castro. He asked them to work to release political prisoners. Then, the United States was holding three Cubans in jail, while Cuba detained two U.S. citizens.

The resulting negotiations resulted in a prisoner exchange, one of the first moves in improving relations between the two countries.

Like any nation's history, Cuba's is complicated. Ordinary people who are interested in contemporary Cuba should inform themselves further. Coming to fast conclusions on any topic, for that matter, does not serve anyone well. The discipline of inquiry and study is not replaced by fast-breaking news.

Mimi Keller's family lived toward the end of the street, three houses from the mall, on our side of the street. The two-story house was designed by her father, Adrian Keller, a quiet, intelligent man who worked as an engineer downtown. It is a beautiful, midcentury home with quality wood, brick, and workmanship everywhere. The Kellers had six children. Mimi and her brother Joel were the youngest and home.

After Mimi came knocking, we planned for my visit. I walked to her house. We played Twister on the family room floor. I remember hands and feet trying to match the right primary colored dots, and then trying to hold the position. Marilyn Keller sat at the kitchen table, playing solitaire, drinking coffee, and smoking cigarettes. It was not dinner time, so meal preparations were not in process. During late afternoons at our house, my mother dispensed glasses of orange juice and a vitamin.

A mother was nearby. That was comforting.

Among her many talents, Marilyn Keller knit afghans and sewed. A sewing machine was usually out of its carrying case and on one end of the family room table. From the time I met her until her last years, she volunteered at a nursing home.

She was an affable woman. Over the years, she certainly loved and encouraged me. During the late 1980s, when I was living and working as a freelance reporter in Puerto Rico, we were in contact again, through Mimi. Marilyn and Adrian visited me while they were vacationing there. They saw my apartment and furnishings. There was no judgment about how I was living, even though I was materially poor at the time. They were happy that I was employed part-time at United Press International. At thirty, I should've been at a better place economically, according to whoever makes the rules for unmarried Cuban American middle-class women working to establish themselves as writers.

I drove them to the San Juan airport in a $500 yellow VW bug. I parked the car under a royal poinciana tree, near my apartment on Las Palomas Street. The car had a large hole on the floor in front of the passenger's seat. Cats liked to climb in to sleep on the seats. I was embarrassed about the car, but Marilyn and Adrian Keller got inside of it as if they were getting into a Cadillac. They appreciated the lift to the airport. I cherish a photograph of Marilyn and me with the VW in the background.

Not long after we moved to Belmont Lane, my father was asked to give a guitar concert at the Kellers' house. It was a great way for the neighbors to get to know him and learn a little about our culture. Peg Schmidt, who lived at the top of the street with her husband and ten children, learned my father would be playing. A classical music buff, she came to hear him.

At the time, he was taking lessons from the guitarist Michael Hauser. My father appeared at the Kellers' with his Spanish classical guitar and a foot stand. He took the opportunity to give a lesson. "What's this?" he asked, referring to the foot stand. He illustrated its use. Mimi remembers the small audience was mesmerized.

My father has the softest hands. His nails are well-kept, like his moustache, in fact, like his entire person. Then, he was soft-spoken, a gentleman, Mimi writes, "exactly the way he is today!"

No strangers to classical music, the Kellers had an organ in their living room. Mimi played it. I lacked musical talent; her abilities impressed me.

In turn, Mimi came to our house to play. There, she encountered some differences. In our house, a *sofrito,* a sauté of green peppers, garlic, onion, and olive oil, was made daily. She writes,

> that smell—that putrid, rank, sharp smell that was the worst I had ever smelled in my life. I remember poking my head around the wall to look inside the pot . . . green peppers cooking? Disgusting, I thought. Plus, it was creating extra steam in the kitchen. The windows above the sink were covered in steam. Time and time again at your house there was that smell and that hot steam. After a few years I got used to it, but I still thought it was rank. . . . Today, when I smell green peppers boiling or frying, it is one of the most entrancing smells I know. They represent a cultural phenomenon, an entire world that was foreign but that I was privileged to know and embrace and be embraced by.

Mimi remembers my mother's lips were painted beautifully in red; in the kitchen she almost always wore an apron. Like my aunt, my mother preferred dresses. She rarely wore pants or shorts.

Our great-aunt and uncle had moved nearby again, this time renting a second-floor apartment in one of two blond brick buildings between Eldridge and Burke, two streets joined by a foot path. My brothers and I often walked to their apartment, and our playmates were welcomed there.

Epifanio rode to Twin City Meats with my father. Great-aunt Carmen sewed for a few neighborhood women. They appreciated her skill and paid for the labor without complaint. In addition, she made beautiful decorative pillows which were sold at Marshall Fields at the mall. Both she and my mother hoped Mimi would learn Spanish. They bestowed praise whenever she pronounced a word correctly. They were good-natured, Mimi said, not pushy about her becoming fluent.

Today, Mimi and her family live in Miami, Florida. She uses Spanish on a regular basis.

The neighborhood women expressed an interest in learning Spanish. So my mother held a class at our home one night a week. Marilyn Keller was a student. I remember the women sitting at our dining room table in the evening, the lamp on overhead. My mother sat at the table's head, where my father sat on more formal occasions.

In 1968, my mother registered for a spring term Spanish literature class at Macalester College. A Spanish professor there, Dr. Fabian, encouraged the Cubans he knew to sign up for classes in order to become certified to teach in the public or private schools.

Keti Beguiristain had registered for the program and suggested my mother do the same. Keti became certified. She taught Spanish language at Regina High School in Minneapolis, and at Derham Hall, Visitation Academy, and St. Thomas Academy in St. Paul.

Meanwhile, at St. Rose of Lima, no classmates befriended me until the fourth grade, when we played softball during gym class. Traditionally, sports have facilitated the integration of different ethnic communities. Lynn Hutmaker, who lived in a big white house near the corner of Skillman Avenue, took a risk. Her older sister LeeAnn was also a friend. The Hutmaker family welcomed me.

Part of the reason for the few friendships among classmates was that the Veigas went home for lunch, since it was a half block away. On the days my mother had to be elsewhere during lunchtime, we carried our lunches in brown paper bags. I hated those days and complained to my mother. But there was no choice. Our lunches were packed—often a baloney sandwich on white bread and a snack. We bought a little carton of milk in the cafeteria for a nickel. I ate alone. I never saw my brothers at school. I didn't look for them.

One day at lunch I was alone at the table in the cafeteria. Lunch was over and the other students were in the playground. A kind teacher encouraged me outside to play. It was more than a suggestion when it came from an elder. Out I went.

During the winter, the playground, whether at lunch or for recess, was a problem for everyone: it was cold. Many children huddled where two walls of the school building intersected. One child was right in the corner, the warmest one. Then kids would gather around him or her, pushing against one another to keep warm. The ones closest to the building took the force of the rhythmic pushing. I'm surprised we didn't squeeze the air out of someone's lungs.

I wore boots to school and carried a plastic shoe case with a zipper; inside were regular shoes for the classroom. That was the style for girls then.

St. Rose of Lima was good enough to hire a speech therapist to help me overcome my Spanish accent in the English language. I don't remember the exercises or the sessions. However, I recall being taken from the classroom to meet with someone in an office near the cafeteria. Today, St. Rose of Lima offers an enrichment program in Spanish for all its students. I see only good things for students acquiring a second language, no matter which one it is.

St. Rose third-grade girls learned to purl and knit. My great-aunt was pleased as she could knit beautifully. She helped me at home as my fingers fumbled with light blue acrylic yarn and the metal needles. I made one scarf. It was long, evidence that I kept at it, but oddly shaped, its edges serrated like a bread knife.

About that time I caught myself daydreaming at school, wondering what it would be like to inhabit the body of another person. What was it like to be the teacher? What was life like for that boy? I didn't share the thoughts.

As an adult reviewing these childhood thoughts, I wonder if they arose as a result of being so marginalized. Or were they signs of a personality disorder?

More than likely, it was the recognition of empathy. I like to believe the imagining of other people's lives was evidence of early literary interest.

My parents made sure we had books to read. I have a copy of *Heidi*. It's a good story. The Bobbsey Twins series by Laura Lee Hope was full of adventure. The Boxcar Children stories by Gertrude Chandler Warner were another favorite. The children managed to live in a boxcar! That was one place we had yet to live.

In recent years, a few architects with environmental concerns have designed fantastic homes using old shipping containers. I haven't convinced my husband that they'd be great for our next home.

I loved the well-crafted Trixie Belden books by Julie Campbell Tatham. The curly-haired, tomboyish Trixie was a great one to follow. She relied on inductive and deductive reasoning but listened to her intuition to solve mysteries. She wiggled out of trouble. Ultimately, Trixie was celebrated by family and friends. I longed to be like her.

At the Roseville public library we earned the privilege of borrowing books. The library, on Hamline Avenue and County Road B, was too far to walk to from our house. Juan Carlos remembers the much-loved library. His favorite books were on the animal kingdom, though he liked other science and biology books too. Every week, my mother drove us there, encouraged by the fact that her children loved to read, just like she and my father. To this day, a library, no matter what size, is a place of comfort.

The Roseville public library adapted to suburban growth and added on to the building. Eventually, it was razed. A new library appeared on the same lot. That one met a similar fate and was rebuilt in 2010. Today the library has more than 340,000 volumes in its collection. Only the library in downtown St. Paul is bigger, with about 400,000 volumes. Roseville has the busiest library in Minnesota.

One day when I was nine years old, I was cutting through a neighbor's front yard, chasing a brother or a friend. I came to the yard at the side of our house. A thought stopped me. I heard it clearly. I wanted to be a writer. With that in mind, I ran to the backyard, toward whomever I'd been chasing, to whatever might prove interesting.

West Belmont Lane was overloaded with children.

At the top of the street, the Schmidts' large house was home to ten children. Tough little Ricky was the one to be reckoned with. He and his friends built a large boys' fort in their backyard. Kids in that fort pelted Juan Carlos one day as he walked home from school. After that event, he'd run past the Schmidts' house to avoid another ambush.

Next, the Higgins had two studious boys; Terrence was a classmate. The Medveds, two doors up from us, had five. Janice Miller was alone with her parents across the street. The Rempels had two, though older. The Luckman family had a boy named Scott. The Wusslers had five—one of them, Janet, became a close friend. The Wellies had six, all boys, the Kellers had six, the McGinnitys had nine. Mary, who was my age, became a friend.

Sometimes children gathered at the street that fed into Belmont Lane when it turned to become, for a short block, North Pascal Avenue. During the summer, people came around with a traveling puppet show and parked their trailer there. Free, regular, outdoor puppet shows—what a treat!

Because there were so many families with children and they knew one another, adult supervision was almost nonexistent. We discovered other worlds as we pedaled our bicycles to other streets. The only rule was that we had to return to our homes when the streetlights turned on. It was a fair arrangement and we complied.

The Veiga children were like regular Minnesotans. We jumped into piles of raked leaves. I liked peeling the bark off the birch tree in the front yard. We crunched through early snow on Halloween, dressed as hobos or ghosts, carrying pillowcases to hold our treats. At home, we sorted the treats as an adult watched, tossing unwrapped candies. Apples were dangerous, as someone might have buried razor blades in them.

One winter, Juan Carlos cut his knee on the jagged remains of a flagpole while sledding in the backyard. We made snow tunnels, slid on ice patches on our way to and from school. We pulled sleds to the hills of snow made by the plows that had cleared the mall's parking lot. We filled balloons with water and hung them with fishing line from the branches of the backyard tree. We loved their frozen shapes. We sucked on icicles fallen from the gutters.

Mary, Janet, Mimi, and I formed a secret club. Boys were excluded. We took wood from our parents' garages to build a two-story fort at the side of our backyard tree. Its first floor was the ground. Its ceiling was made of two boards to form a square hole; from it we climbed to the next floor, our lookout.

Juan Carlos, who had started first grade at St. Rose, was friendly with neighbors Michael and Tim Medved. They too built a fort in their backyard. Eventually, both forts were raided for wood. No formal accusations were made but we had our suspicions. They were confirmed as we saw an expansion on the large fort in the Schmidts' yard.

Second grade was memorable for Juan Carlos as a result of dashed hopes for a good Kris Kringle gift. He had taken time to choose a gift for the classmate whose name he had drawn. Whoever picked his name had given him a few ugly crayon-colored pictures. He cried for the unfairness of the exchange. He was angry with the child who thought Juan was a girl's name, or so he reasoned. Our mother went to school to talk with the teacher, who apologized for what had happened. She bought a nice replacement gift.

What I remember most vividly about Juan Carlos's Roseville years was his large collection of plastic zoo animals. There wasn't a domesticated animal among them. They lived at our great-aunt and uncle's apartment. I played with them there, where his siblings and their friends wouldn't destroy or scatter them. Every week, our great-aunt bought Juan Carlos a new animal for the collection.

Juan Carlos showed artistic talent. He liked to paint. My mother enrolled him in a children's painting class at the St. Paul Science Museum, now the Science Museum of Minnesota. He moved through the ranks quickly as the teachers recognized his talent and skill level. He surpassed beginners and intermediate students. One oil painting of a raging forest fire won him honorable mention in a class with college students and adults. The painting, too, was a treasure kept at our great-aunt's apartment until she died.

By the time Luis Gustavo was in the sixth grade, he was playing a six-string guitar from Sears, Roebuck and Company. It cost $19. A St. Rose of Lima teacher who was a native of Trinidad, Cyril Paul, invited Luis to join an ensemble. They played at the school Mass on the first Friday of every month.

Often, my mother sent me to buy bread at the grocery store at the mall. Unfortunately, many times I returned with a crushed loaf, as I tossed the bread inside a baby stroller. Typically, a friend was along. We'd stash our jackets on top of the bread to ease our walks around the mall. Its large center hallway made it a great place to roam, especially in winter. A promotional table or an antique show display was sometimes set up. Once, I was given a free Smokey the Bear stuffed toy along with the message that I had the power to prevent forest fires.

St. Rose of Lima third graders prepared to receive another sacrament, Confirmation. We'd become soldiers of Christ. By doing so, we were alerted that we could expect hard times because of our beliefs. A symbolic slap on my face would remind me of future difficulties. Confirmation meant we were maturing as Christians. We said yes to continuing on the journey of faith.

Like everyone in the congregation, I would renew the promises my parents and godparents made for me during my baptism in Cuba. Faith was being passed on. I chose a sponsor, but I don't remember who that was. Students selected confirmation names, which would be added after our middle names. The name should belong to a saint we admired. I anguished when it came time to submit it, initially settling on Marie, a version of Mary's name, which my mother approved.

Even so, Marie didn't sound right. Of course not: it was an anglicized Maria. I knew Marie wouldn't sound odd when it was called aloud in church. More and more I wanted to fit in, as children normally want to do. I didn't discuss the problem with anyone. By then, I had asked my mother for permission to dye my hair blonde. She did not give it.

In the end, though I struggled, I am glad to see I overcame a cultural difference without bending to peer approval. Maria won over Marie. I became a soldier of Christ, confirmed Marisella Lourdes Maria Veiga, named for the Blessed Mother three times.

Confirmation day came. The bishop anointed my forehead with oil, said my new name, and added that I would be sealed with the gift of the Holy Spirit.

A few years later, the sacrament was delayed for Catholic children until seventh grade, another change resulting from the Second Vatican Council.

I fell in love twice in third grade. My first love was a Boston terrier who lived at the end of Belmont Lane with its owners, the Nerhaugens. When the dog was chained outside near the open garage door and I happened to be on the way to the mall or going to my great-aunt and uncle's apartment, I stopped to pet it. Its huge eyes, large forehead, small size, and gentle disposition—I loved that dog.

I also developed a crush on a television star, Burt Ward, who played Robin on *Batman*. He was indispensable to Adam West, who starred as Batman. The action series was based on the comic book character. On Wednesday nights my brothers, Mimi Keller, and I went to my great-aunt and uncle's apartment to watch the program. We were dedicated.

While there, Mimi practiced Spanish. My great-uncle didn't say much, though he did speak some English. He read books and newspapers in a comfortable chair at the far end of the living room near the windows, away from the television set. About this time, we gave our great-aunt and uncle nicknames: Tilly and Dino. My siblings and I still refer to our great-aunt Carmen as Tilly when we speak of her, which is often.

My mother may have found the evidence of my secret crush on Robin. After all, she folded sheets and towels and stored them in the linen closet. That was where I hid Robin's color portrait—the size of a bubblegum trading card. In it, Robin wore his crime-fighting costume. I'd pull the picture from its hiding place, look at it, and return it quickly.

Years later, as a young woman in Miami, I went to a car show in Miami Beach. Robin was there in full costume, showing the Batmobile. His skin was very white, like cornstarch. The actor played such a tired role, I thought, and my sympathy went to him.

Another favorite was a spy show, *The Man from U.N.C.L.E.*, with Napoleon Solo, the American, and Illya Kuryakin, a Russian.

Having matured a little, in fourth grade I developed a crush on a singer, Davy Jones of the Monkees. The television show was about the band and its shenanigans, though their music was also featured. For preteen girls, the band members were the draw. Mimi, Janet, Mary, and I were big fans. We took turns watching the show at our houses. We listed favorites. Davy was most attractive for his looks and British accent. Micky was next, then Peter and then, finally, the quiet one, Michael. Sometimes Micky exchanged places with Davy.

We bought their 45s and hit albums. We memorized their songs. We read about them in *Tiger Beat* magazine. Teenagers and young adults were crazy about the Beatles, but we were too young to appreciate them. Instead, we went hog-wild for the Monkees.

One day, I swore, I would meet them.

Finally, when I was about twenty, a man I dated learned of this childhood infatuation. Davy Jones and Micky Dolenz played at a nightclub in North Miami Beach. He bought two tickets to a show.

Afterward, I grabbed the piece of cardboard advertising drink specials that was set in the middle of the cocktail table. I wanted autographs, so I went to the hotel lobby. When it was my turn to ask for autographs, I handed over the folded cardboard and pen. I confessed to Davy that once upon a time I'd been madly in love with him.

He looked at me for a few seconds, perhaps to gauge my age, then signed his name. He didn't say a word.

Mimi's mother and mine agreed their daughters should learn a little poise. Were we too tomboyish? Was it the fort we built? The all-day bike riding? Without our consent or expression of interest, they signed us up for ballet classes at Andahazy School of Classical Ballet on Grand Avenue.

Lorand Andahazy and Anna Adrianova Andahazy taught the pre-Soviet Russian method of ballet. The two had been members of the Russian ballet. They moved to St. Paul in 1945, opening the school in 1947. The classes were on Saturday mornings in a studio above a former restaurant. I wore a black long-sleeved leotard with black tights and black slippers. Mimi had a short-sleeved leotard, black slippers, and pink tights, which I coveted. She looked better.

Ballet was serious business, so we paid attention. Lorand Andahazy often taught with his heavily accented English. I was used to hearing English spoken with an accent; I had one myself. However, his English was rough, guttural, and loud. He wasn't someone you hugged after class. He was a gymnast and equestrian before becoming a classical dancer. Training respectful girls was easier than breaking horses, but he still raised his voice, at times, in frustration.

We walked into the studio quietly, stopping to rub the bottoms of our leather slippers in the chalk box to limit sliding on the wooden floor. After that ritual, we claimed a place at the bar. Someone played the piano. We did our bar exercises carefully. The teacher made adjustments at the bar or from the front of the room.

The second half of the class was when we left the bar to perform lessons on the floor. This was the time for heightened frustration for everyone involved. Not always, but sometimes, when Mr. Andahazy saw errors, he spoke to us about them loudly, in Russian.

His wife, Anna Adrianova, was a talented ballerina and teacher. Besides the plies and spins and foot and arm positions, she taught us to curtsey at the end of class. It is a beautiful way for dancers to show appreciation for an audience's love of the work they are doing on stage. I am moved by it.

Doing well in ballet was important. I asked my father to install a practice bar for me at home. He secured a wooden bar along a basement wall. It was near the washer and dryer area where, a week or two earlier, I had found my dolls defaced. Someone had drawn moustaches on them. No matter how I tried, they wouldn't come off. I was upset. The unidentified vandal remains at large.

Soon, I realized ballet had become more important than the dolls. Maybe it was time to put them away, I reasoned. I was growing up and getting a sense of it.

Without music, I did bar exercises. In addition, I practiced turns so I wouldn't be embarrassed when we were required to turn across the floor on Saturdays. Neither Mimi nor I starred in the class. But we learned to appreciate the dance and gained greater exposure to classical music.

Our parents bought us tickets to see a production of the Andahazy Ballet Company. I was excited. I felt a little more grown up as Mimi and I walked into the auditorium to find our seats. In Cuba, my grandmother, great-aunt, and mother bought tickets to the ballet once a year. In St. Paul, they kept the custom.

I began knowing a little bit more about my mother during this time. For one thing, she disliked large houses. I remember her driving by a house she and my father had considered when they were house-hunting.

Too big, she said, two floors. She liked our Roseville house. I overheard her tell another adult that the basement, which no one had in Cuba or in Miami, was a good feature. The children could make a mess in the basement. No adults had to look at the chaos if they happened to drop by without notice, not uncommon with Cubans.

The basement was especially important as a playroom during the winter. Luis had his own room in the basement. There was nothing to be scared of there, unlike in the Dayton Avenue house.

The black-and-white TV was downstairs. Sometimes we watched a Spanish language instruction show on KTCA called *Ya Hablamos Español.* Howard Hathaway starred as Spanish-language teacher Don Miguel. Our family knew him, as did most of the Minnesota Cubans. For a few months, Keti Beguiristain had worked for him. By way of this show, he introduced the Spanish language and customs to more than 150,000 Minnesotans and others in the Upper Midwest.

Sometimes, Noris Beruvides had small parts on his show. One time, she remembers, she played a nurse and helped teach medical vocabulary.

One of the benefits of exile is that people are forced out of comfort zones. New skills are learned or developed because there's a need. It is similar to when one has to make a living doing work one is not naturally inclined to do. This "having to do it" helps people develop in unexpected ways. People develop confidence in their self-reliance.

In Roseville, I learned a lesson about marriage from my mother. I sat next to her in the station wagon. As she turned the car into the driveway, she passed on some advice.

"Marry an American," she said, stopping the car. "They help you more around the house."

On Saturdays, Mr. Medved babysat the children so his wife could leave the house and visit other family or go out to lunch with a friend. Another American husband did the same.

I didn't say anything.

This was the first time I recall my mother talking to me about my future. I would grow up and have a husband and have children too. I didn't want that future. I was having too much fun, unlike the adults—the only fun they seemed to have was sitting around talking with one another.

Nevertheless, because it was such an unusual remark, I squirreled the piece of advice away. I married an American.

St. Rose of Lima school signaled other signs of strange future developments. I believe I was in fourth grade when parents were consulted about the sex education videos to be shown on two evenings at the school. The first night was parents' preview. The next evening, my mother told me to walk up to the school to see a short movie in the cafeteria.

The characters in the film were line drawings, cartoons. A narrator gave information that I didn't understand or ignored. There was a drawing of a married couple sitting on a sofa, talking.

What did I learn? When my parents talked on the living room sofa, I should leave them alone. That was fine with me. It was easy. I had never seen my parents sitting on the sofa talking. My father was either at work or doing outdoor chores at home. My mother was cooking, folding wash, or running errands. However, I resolved to be considerate if I saw the behavior. I would leave them alone.

The film contained information about the menstrual cycle, which I didn't understand. Was it lack of language ability or the newness of the information? No adult followed up with a discussion at home. My parents didn't discuss bodies or sexuality. St. Rose of Lima prepared students for what was coming naturally and inevitably. Our bodies would change. Like it or not, children became adults.

I didn't want any part of it.

Instead, like tropical summers that lasted forever, I wanted my great-aunt to continue sewing our clothes or knitting our sweaters, to keep cooking good meals at her apartment. I wanted to continue reading the books my mother let me choose off the library shelves or buy at Target.

Meanwhile, I could help a little with my younger brother and sister. Glenna is left-handed, but no one else in the family was left-handed. I took on the task of teaching her to write with her right hand, even though she had not yet started kindergarten. Left-handed Mimi remembers that as a child I was careful about printing and handwriting. She tried to imitate me in this regard.

By this time, I was old enough for another kind of pet. A hamster caught my attention at a pet store in the mall. The hamster's size and fur are right for a child's hands. My parents bought it along with the required accoutrements: cage, litter, food pellets, water bottle, and exercise wheel. I loved its beady eyes and tiny paws. I was amazed by how much food it stored in its cheeks. I named the creature Lucky.

It escaped from its cage a few times. How the escapades happened remains a mystery. Once the hamster was gone for so long we thought it was dead. But then, my mother was woken in the middle of the night—Lucky stood at her feet. My father caught it.

The creature's luck ran out, however, when my siblings and/or one of their friends got hold of it. Perhaps the stress of tossing and catching the hamster killed it. I wasn't in the basement when it happened.

I mourned Lucky's death, burying it in a shoe box at the edge of the backyard beneath a bush. Once again, death. It had come to a classmate at St. Mark's. Each of my two pets had died.

"Vengan a tomar el jugo!" Those words belong to my mother calling us inside the house for orange juice and a vitamin tablet at about four o'clock in the afternoon.

Summer weekends swimming at Lake Josephine and Turtle Lake, I loved those days. I couldn't wait to be old enough to swim to the raft and dive from it, like the big kids. At Como Park, two elegant white swans glided on the lake. I loved going there to see them.

Janet invited me on company picnics with her family. Her father, Robert Wussler, worked for St. Paul Publishing and her mother, Mary Pat Wussler, worked for a hotel and banquet catering company. One picnic was held at Como Park Zoo. That time we left the area for carnival rides that were permanently installed on the zoo's grounds. We weren't reprimanded.

Kathy, Janet's oldest sister, managed a dental office. She had a car and often took us to Dairy Queen or McDonald's during the summer. Janet's brother Jack, who was closest to us in age, spent time on the McGinnitys' driveway, looking under a car hood, trying to understand motors. Besides Patrick McGinnity, one of the Wellie twins was usually there. They'd talk and then someone would lean into the motor and stay under the hood.

I wondered what they were doing and why none of the girls followed suit. They didn't invite us to look. The boys shared little jokes among themselves. We didn't understand them. We girls had our territory; they had theirs.

I spent many days in the Wusslers' basement playing card games—Go Fish or Crazy Eights. We played backyard croquet. We talked at their spotless kitchen table. I can see Jack or Bobby making lunch. Neither of my brothers did that.

Bobby was the oldest son. He was a quiet young man who liked to sit in a chair and rock, especially while watching television. That was unusual but everyone accepted it. Likewise, though I was different, the Wusslers welcomed me.

Marriage, company jobs, housework, motors, parents talking on the couch—I didn't understand why I had to learn about these matters.

In 1967, the new church at St. Rose of Lima was finished, an architecturally modern structure that remains in use today. Vatican II results were visible. Women no longer covered their heads inside the sanctuary. We discarded lacy veils. Many stopped buying Easter bonnets, though I liked choosing and wearing mine. Many girls and young women wore miniskirts. From the pulpit, a priest asked we not wear them to Mass.

In contrast to the new, modern ways being adopted by the church, I was fascinated by a particular Servite who caught my attention when I played near the top of the street after school. Dressed in full habit with black robes falling to her ankles, she walked in front of the school from one end of the sidewalk to the other. Her fingers handled rosary beads. She did this every afternoon.

With nine children, the McGinnity household was active. My friend Mary McGinnity had a November birthday. She invited me over to celebrate it and her mother made hot dish. It was the first time I had eaten it; it was delicious.

Mrs. McGinnity was a housewife; her husband was a city bus driver. He was cheerful if my aunt and I had the good fortune of having him as our driver when we caught the bus home after a shopping trip downtown. It was good to be recognized in public in a positive way, to not be met with silence.

The summer of 1967, our family took a long drive in the station wagon to Miami. We were going to see my paternal grandparents and their daughter Rosita, my father's only sibling. She was visiting from Mexico, where she and her husband and three children had gone into exile.

Our grandmother Manuela lived with us at the time. She shared a bedroom with Juan Carlos. Luis moved to a basement room. There were four kids and three adults on a three-day drive to Miami.

Aunt Rosita had asked for gift ideas. I requested a pair of maracas, a choice resulting from my infatuation with the Monkees. She brought me a beautiful pair. I didn't need music lessons to learn to play them so they gave me hours of fun.

Six months later, on January 6, 1968, my aunt Rosita died in Mexico City due to complications in childbirth. She had gone into labor on New Year's and was admitted to the capital's best clinic. However, because of the holiday, the hospital was understaffed. The employees had left for end-of-year celebrations. She needed a blood transfusion. There wasn't any blood available.

The baby also died. Besides her husband, Rafael Alvarez, she left two boys, Bernardo and Rafael, and a girl, Lourdes.

I was in the tub with water running, sitting close to the faucet to feel the falling warm water. My mother answered the telephone in my bedroom, which was directly across the hall.

She started wailing. I had never heard her cry like that before, so I turned off the water to hear more clearly. Only death could cause this, I thought. Perhaps her mother had died. Grandmother Manuela had left our house and returned to her son Homero's house in Valencia, Venezuela. She was old, I reasoned. I sat in the tub listening.

My mother called my great-aunt Carmen to relate the news. I heard her say it would be horrible to tell my father Rosita had died, along with the child she carried. I was told when I came out of the bathroom.

My siblings and I went to visit our great-aunt and uncle that afternoon. When my father returned from work to a house devoid of children, he'd immediately know something was wrong. My mother shared the devastating news.

When we returned that evening, I found a tissue in the living room, no doubt my father's tears drying on it. The tissue was the only evidence of his sorrow. I never saw him cry until later years, when unfortunately and inevitably, other sorrows came along.

One winter Sunday evening, I had a taste of heaven. It comes when you least expect it. It lasts a little while. Not long. A few moments. What's important is that you stop and recognize it. By doing so, for a few seconds, you find yourself in perfect balance, in perfect peace. Contentment is indeed possible.

No matter how you try, you can't manufacture it. A taste of heaven is a gift from God.

Our family was returning from visiting another family, probably the Lauers. Like American Southerners, Cubans are big on visiting people. We don't wait for holidays to gather.

My father drove the station wagon and my mother was in the passenger seat. I was in the third seat, a pop-up which faced the rear window.

The night sky had millions of stars. We were going home. The fields were quiet and beautiful with snow, snow that hadn't been trampled. I felt perfect peace. I was happy.

Sometime late that spring, my father was contacted by a first cousin, Oscar Fernández, then president of South American Hardwood in Miami. In Cuba, my father had worked for Oscar's father, José Fernández, who was married to his aunt Clara Veiga.

He got an offer he couldn't refuse.

Rosita's death was another factor influencing the decision to move south. My grandparents mourned as their only daughter had died. From my aunt's death until her own, my grandmother Eva, for the most part, wore the traditional colors of mourning, black and gray and white. Occasionally she'd wear a pale pink blouse.

The summer following the Miami vacation, I finished fifth grade. It was 1968. I learned we were moving to, not just going on vacation to, Miami. This was terrible news. Why did we have to move again? We had friends and liked our school.

Our last evening in Minnesota, the Beruvides family invited us to dinner at their place in Sibley Manor. My grandmother was back from Venezuela, no doubt to help with the move. My great-aunt and uncle were there. They would move to Florida as well.

Ariana Beruvides shared photographs documenting that evening. If she hadn't, I would have not remembered our last night in Minnesota.

At fifty-seven, my grandmother Manuela smiles for Roberto Beruvides, who is the photographer. She is pretty: her black hair is brushed back. It is graying. She wears dangling earrings. Her blue-and-white vertical striped summer dress is outlined in red piping. A purse hangs on her arm. Her older sister, my great-aunt Carmen, is demure in a brocade dress, sitting with legs carefully crossed. Her hair is almost all gray as she is already sixty. She wears silver and gray cat-eye glasses.

My father wears plaid shorts, a rare sight. He has dark-framed glasses, black hair, and a trimmed moustache. His chest and shoulders are strong from lifting weights. My mother is thin, with short wavy hair. She wears a matching pant and sleeveless top outfit. The shell has a paisley design on the front. Noris Beruvides is petite and lovely, with dark brown wavy hair and huge brown eyes.

Two other photographs document that last evening. One stars a group of Cuban children whose identities were being shaped by living formative years in Minnesota. José, Ariana, Luis, Juan Carlos, and me—we are among the first exiled Cuban children brought way far north of their native island. Glenna and Robertico are under five years old in the photograph—among the first Cubans born in Minnesota.

As my father reflects on our family's experience in Minnesota, he says, "It was a good place for us, even with the cold weather. It was a good way for us to get to know the customs and its many facets. Assimilation is quicker for the children. We would not have learned these things having stayed in Miami."

Luis had finished seventh grade, I had finished fifth grade, Juan Carlos had finished third grade. Glenna would start school in Miami that fall. She went as a fully bilingual kindergartener who helped her Spanish-speaking public school teacher with English.

I didn't want to leave Minnesota. Again, no choice.

The house sold. Luis Beguiristain bought my father's VW for $300. The Mayflower moving truck came for our furnishings. We packed a few suitcases to take along in the station wagon.

The drive to Miami took three days. Yes, we could choose the hotels we stayed in according to their swimming pools. Goodbye Belmont Lane. Goodbye Minnesota.

And then, once again, we were gone.

On September 26, 1974, my mother died of cancer in Miami, Florida.

A few years later, in 1977, I returned to Minnesota as a transfer student to Macalester College. Besides being keen on furthering my education, I sought the comfort of a place where my family had been intact, where the home they represented was whole.

Minnesota was a place where we lived that reality. The physical evidence of the places my family lived had not vanished. I could renew contact with a few people I knew from my childhood.

Even so, I learned that while landmarks remained, the stable home of my past was gone.

There is no single place to which I can attach the importance of all that has been.

—Ivy Slovak in *A Mother's Love* by Mary Morris

CHAPTER 7

Paul D. Bethel was among the early supporters of my desire to become a professional writer. He died the winter of 1979, during my last semester at Macalester College. By then, I had read parts of his book *The Losers: The Definitive Report, by an Eyewitness, of the Communist Conquest of Cuba and the Soviet Penetration in Latin America* for a history class on Mexico and the Caribbean. Bethel was a press officer for the U.S. Embassy in Havana until relations with Cuba ended in 1961. His Cuban wife, Diana González de Bethel, also cheered me on.

The Bethels, their son Eric, Diana's youngest sister Maria Eugenia, and a St. Bernard lived a few blocks down the street from us in the northern part of Coconut Grove, Florida. Their home was open to friends of all ages and cultures. As a result, their living room and backyard swimming pool were active. You never knew who you'd meet at the Bethels, other neighborhood kids included. Grandmother Manuela, Juan Carlos, Glenna, and I visited or sometimes went along on one of their activities. The Bethels founded *Aboard*, a bilingual in-flight trade publication serving seven Latin American countries. They offered me a job with the magazine after I graduated from college. Somehow, everyone assumed I would return to Miami. So did I.

However, my academic advisor and English professor Roger Blakely didn't make assumptions about my future. He stopped me in the hallway outside his office one spring afternoon. His door stayed open way beyond a professor's required office hours. Opera blasted into the hallway. Roger Blakely was enthusiastic about the humanities and about encouraging students to explore them. He lived what he loved. That's what he did. Early one semester he started painting with oils. He brought the small first works on canvas into the office and displayed them on the wall. He asked what I thought of them. Then, he asked another question after I told him about my job offer.

"Are you sure that's what you want to do?"

"Yes," I said. "I know the publishers. They even said I could work there part-time if I wanted. I want to write poetry."

Blakely looked at me from across his desk. He didn't press. Sometimes, I wish he had, though he didn't believe in "meddling" in other people's lives. Once he asked why it was important for me to make so many decisions about my siblings' lives, especially when they were at such a distance. I didn't understand this proclivity as a cultural difference at that time; therefore, I couldn't explain my behavior.

Other important events transpired that spring term. The Islamic Revolution of 1979 was one. On January 16, the Shah of Iran, Mohammad Reza Shah Pahlavi, went into exile. He was the last Persian monarch. A few weeks later, on February 1, the Ayatollah Khomeini returned to Iran from his own exile. On April 1, the country held a referendum that changed its direction—Iran became an Islamic republic.

Many of my Macalester friends were international students from Iran. I felt as comfortable with the Persians as I did with other Hispanics, even if they hailed from Mexico, Colombia, Puerto Rico, or the United States. The only slight barrier to total comfort with the Persians, at times, was language, as I did not speak Farsi. I didn't mind their speaking Farsi among themselves when I was present. They weren't necessarily talking about me. Many people have that fear when a language they don't understand is spoken in front of them.

The Persians were good about translation when it was needed. When asked, and they hesitated initially, they taught their non-Farsi-speaking friends a few choice words and expressions. Our short language lessons were laughter-filled. Today I can still repeat the phrases I learned.

With the Shah's exit and the subsequent change in government, the Persian students went into a tailspin, faced with the implications of what the revolution meant for themselves and their family members in Iran. Some confronted altered plans for continuing their education. Furthermore, they had to decide if they would return to live in an Islamic republic or make lives for themselves in the United States or another country.

I understood their alarm. My history contained revolution and recovery. Eventually, our family members accepted lives and deaths in the United States. I could offer a compassionate ear as more news and family advice came from Iran. Enormous changes were taking place. Every Persian's life began shifting.

My closest friend, Fariba Sanikhatam, once the campus president of the International Student Association, would be graduating the following spring. The revolution threatened a postponement of her educational plans. In limbo, the students waited to see what would happen next.

The Persians were so gracious. They included me among their friends and families, even for overnight visits to off-campus friends. More than once, I visited a Persian woman who was in a graduate program at the University of Minnesota. Soheila had a studio apartment in a high-rise in Dinkytown. The place was striking for its floor-to-ceiling windows in the living room area. We shared meals, wine, anguish, confusion, music, and laughter. The Persians shared their stashes of high-quality pistachios; they introduced me to the pomegranate. Because there were several young women in the group, we slept on the carpeted floor. I have never slept on better-quality cotton sheets than those from Iran.

At the time, Fariba was exploring her artistic side by taking a sculpture class. She knew I loved poetry. She read it in Farsi. Everyone listened carefully and loved it. I focused on the rhythm of the language since comprehension was impossible. She tried to translate the poems. After giving it a good try, she sighed and said the poem was so beautiful but its beauty was lost in English. I understood the role of connotation and the inherent difficulty of translation. I'd lived that way since we left Cuba.

By age twenty, I was practiced in living a culturally split life. Childhood experiences with Americans in Minnesota were difficult to explain to Miami Cubans, so I didn't do it. The exile community was so large that some Cubans didn't have more than cursory exchanges, if any, with Americans.

Regularly, I was called on to translate expressions, if not language. This is a normal job for immigrant children. My siblings and I dreaded translating the content of government documents for my grandmother Manuela. Bureaucratic jargon made comprehension in English difficult. So I could relate to Fariba's difficulty in trying to make her Persian-self understood. It's a huge part of the immigrant experience.

Often, the Persian women spoke of their home and the traditions they missed. The city of Shiraz, with its countless flowers, was so well-loved that I swore one day I would visit it. Soheila's name means "spring star." If I ever had a child, I told her, I would give her that name.

Of course, I had American students as friends too, including Minnesotans. Mary Hamburgen, from Rochester, Minnesota, and her roommate Judith Kassel, from Utah, I believe, lived in my dormitory. I met Mary's lifelong friend Midori Okasaki, a history major who visited them regularly from her dorm.

Midori and her family generously opened their home to me and another student, Marcela Espinosa, who was from Colombia. Midori's father, Dr. Haruo Okasaki, was a neuropathologist at the Mayo Clinic. He thought we'd be interested in seeing his lab, so we went over to the clinic one afternoon. I was startled and impressed by the collection of human brains in jars. Some had suffered trauma from a fall; he pointed out the evidence and tapped the glass. One brain had been shot.

Bikhar Okasaki was a nurse at the motherhouse of the Sisters of St. Francis. She was happy for me to meet them, especially the older sisters. She made sure I got to Mass, though at the time I was not practicing.

Midori's maternal grandmother, Ng Yim Chun, or Mrs. Joe Louis in English, lived with the family. I was glad of that because she taught me to make egg drop soup. Midori showed an interest in cooking from early on, and she taught me to make fried rice. These two simple recipes were on my table frequently. They still appear.

I learned to use chopsticks at the Okasaki house at their Thanksgiving Day table.

Meanwhile, I didn't have contact with any Cubans who were part of my early childhood. The Beguiristain family had moved to Texas. José Beruvides was at the University of Minnesota, but I didn't look for him. With the exception of Mimi Keller, I hadn't kept up with Roseville friends.

Mimi attended the University of Minnesota, but she took a quarter off to go out west to work at a national park. She returned to the Twin Cities but then took another quarter off to tour the Midwest as an actor in a theater group.

Marilyn and Adrian Keller, still on West Belmont Lane in Roseville, would come to my rescue if needed. However, I noticed the Keller kids were proud of their self-sufficiency. They made it on their own. I resolved to do likewise, though my father continued to send money for living expenses and books and tuition. I had a scholarship and work-study job at Macalester. My senior year, my grandmother Manuela gave me $1,000 to help with tuition.

That spring of 1979, my first poem, "Miami Beach," was published in *Chanter,* the college's literary magazine. One of Chilean poet Pablo Neruda's poems, "Ode to Some Yellow Flowers," was also published, along with my translation of it. Several of my hand-built ceramic sculptures were in a senior art exhibit. Later, a few pieces were included in an exhibit in a bank lobby in downtown St. Paul. I made my debut as a young writer and visual artist in Minnesota.

My father came to my college graduation from Miami. Luis Gustavo came from Lexington, Kentucky, where he was working as an electrical engineer with IBM.

Unfortunately, I returned to Miami too soon after graduating from college.

While I was away, my father had sold the house in Coconut Grove and bought another in the Silver Bluff neighborhood.

Grandmother Manuela and Glenna shared a bedroom. A third bed didn't fit. My father remained a widower for nine years after my mother's death. His room was across the hall.

Juan Carlos had a bedroom with a bathroom in the back of the house. It was an addition. An extra twin bed was there. To get to this bedroom, you walked past a door leading to the backyard, then a short corridor with windows on its north side. Often, birds would fly at their reflections on the panes. They were frightened. In turn, the bird strikes scared anyone who passed the window. To dissuade them, my father placed several plastic dolls, including an old Barbie or two, on the window sill. We began referring to the back bedroom as the Santeria room, as if the dolls were items that belonged on a sacrificial altar to a Yoruba god.

Juan Carlos planned to continue engineering studies at Bradley University in Illinois and was scheduled to leave that September. In a few short months, the bedroom would be mine.

I started working at *Aboard*, the in-flight magazine, assisting the new editor, David P. Bethel, Paul's son from an earlier marriage.

Soon thereafter, my grandmother Manuela had a mild heart attack. Juan Carlos sped with her to Pan American Hospital with my sister and me in the backseat. She panted and cried out with pain. She survived it.

As the eldest daughter, I realized that this event, which reflected my grandmother's failing health, meant more domestic responsibilities for me. She didn't have the health to continue running a household with young adults and dealing with their problems, many of which she couldn't understand. There was a linguistic, cultural, and generational divide. Simultaneously, she mourned her daughter's death. My grandmother prayed constantly.

No one told me I was required to take on the work. Yet I knew the responsibilities would be mine. It was culturally appropriate.

I didn't want the job; I'd had a taste of it earlier. So without consulting a mature adult, including my father, I quit the magazine, packed a suitcase, and returned to Minnesota.

Fariba Sanikhatam had rented an apartment on Grand Avenue for the summer of 1979. A younger cousin, Coco, was with her. With little money and no job prospects, I joined them. They were hospitable, but I was having a terrible time adjusting to a new phase.

The Lutsen Resort on Lake Superior had openings for servers. More than likely, Mimi's adventure working at national parks out west served as an example. I could wait tables in Lutsen, I concluded. The job was not unreasonable for a young writer. Paul Bethel had worked as a lumberjack in Idaho. Writers and artists worked all kinds of jobs to generate income.

What was more, housing and food were provided. Northern Minnesota offered beauty and quiet, two major draws. During my free time, I would write poetry. It seemed like a good idea, though I wouldn't know a soul.

So, with the little money I had, I bought a one-way Greyhound bus ticket to Lutsen. I could explore new territory but be close enough to friends in the Twin Cities in the case of any emergency. It was an adventure.

At the Lutsen Resort, I was welcomed in a large lobby and shown the dining room. Scandinavian design predominated, as did the view of the lake. The hewn pine paneling, even on the ceiling, was warm and beautiful. In 1952, architect Edwin Lundie had rebuilt the lodge, as the previous one had been destroyed by a fire a year earlier. I was shown to a small room on the top floor and unpacked. The hallway was empty when I went downstairs.

At the dinner table in the kitchen, I met my coworkers. I had never seen a restaurant's kitchen and was amazed by the size of the industrial appliances and work stations.

Afterward, I swam in the indoor pool. The single bed certainly looked appealing that first night. However, once I lay down, it sagged. Not a slight swoop, but a drop. To date, it is the worst bed I have slept in. Even a sleeping bag without an air mattress beneath it inside a tent was better.

The following morning I was trained on how the table-to-kitchen system worked. I went out to the dining room to attend to breakfast and lunch customers. The kind customers left tips, though I was forgetful and full of apologies. I was glad when the shift ended. I went to the pool to swim again and then, when it was time, downstairs to dinner with my coworkers.

Afterward, a coworker invited me to his cabin. Others would be there. I was happy for the company. I sat on the sofa and accepted a can of beer.

The head waitress came into the cabin and sat in a chair across a coffee table to drink a beer too. She was a young, serious woman, strong and fast. She had light brown hair, long, to the waist, and she wore it in a ponytail. I don't remember a smile.

I imagine she rolled her eyes when she heard I was coming from the Cities. She might have thought I wasn't cut out for the job: a recent graduate from Macalester and a Cuban! Why, for heaven's sakes, would I move to Lutsen?

"Could you work tonight? Someone can't come in," she said, reaching forward to rest the beer can on the coffee table.

A young man came into the cabin, opened the door to the refrigerator, and took a beer. He opened it in the kitchen and took a long sip.

I was no stranger to work. I did housework, I worked part-time during my undergraduate years. My body ached. I didn't want to be on my feet for another shift. I wanted to go to bed, as uncomfortable as it was.

Besides, there is a saying that Cubans, as driven as we are, work in order to live. In contrast, Americans live in order to work.

"We need help in the kitchen, with the oven."

"I have to see it again," I said, stalling. Perhaps it wouldn't be too hard, I thought.

We finished our beer and I followed her back to the lodge.

That was when I saw the northern lights. I didn't know what they were or that they even existed. Rays of sunlight were streaming from the stars.

"What's going on?" I'd had only one beer. "Is there a light show?"

"Those are the northern lights," someone answered behind me.

They were wonderful!

Soon we were at the back kitchen door. We went in and I looked at the oven. A woman was working.

I couldn't do it. I'd never seen such an enormous oven. I feared a burn.

"No, I'm sorry. I can't do it."

The head waitress became a refrigerator with a closed door. Underneath, a current was running. She was not dour or sour. She didn't speak.

Standing in that kitchen, I concluded it was in my best interest to leave the job at Lutsen. I lacked friends to help me work through this initial problem. The future looked bleak: no car, no friends, only recalcitrant coworkers. Perhaps I was wrong in thinking they would stonewall me. Since I couldn't pitch in to help them, I reasoned, they wouldn't help me. I resolved to work a few days until I earned enough money in tips to buy a return ticket to the Twin Cities.

Three days later, I waited alone with my suitcase for the Greyhound bus on the side of Highway 61. I was returning to Fariba's apartment as she prepared to move on campus.

Fortunately, underemployment and unemployment made me a good candidate for the federal Comprehensive Employment and Training Act, or CETA, which had been enacted in 1973. My friend and recent Macalester graduate Guadalupe Cervantes, who had landed a job teaching art at a public elementary school, alerted me to the program. Thankfully, I qualified. I was placed in a full-time position as a reading assistant with a remedial program at Humboldt Senior High School in West St. Paul.

Shortly thereafter, Fariba moved. Her cousin Coco left to go to college elsewhere. Without my asking, the Bilial family—a husband, wife, and sister-in-law—invited me to live with them. They were African American Muslims who were friendly with Fariba. I'm sure she shared her concerns about my welfare. They offered me a basement room until I saved enough for a deposit for my own apartment. I remain grateful for their hospitality.

I packed my sole suitcase again and moved to their house from Grand Avenue. My bed was a sleeping bag on the floor and I had lots of blankets. Bus transportation was easy from the Bilial house. The only migraine headache I've had was formed and relieved in their basement.

Once I had enough money for a deposit and first month's rent, I moved to an old and roomy duplex on Laurel Avenue, in the Merriam Park neighborhood. In keeping with my earlier pattern, I don't remember the move. More than likely, the Bilial family drove me and my suitcase. I didn't own anything else.

Upstairs, the duplex had two bedrooms and a bathroom. Downstairs, the kitchen had a large sink with a window above it. There was an adjacent dining area. A carpeted living room was near the front door. A half bath downstairs didn't work so that door stayed closed. Rent was cheap; heat was included.

The place looked a little grimy, but it was my own. I was glad to have a place and a job that paid well enough so I could afford it. I bought a used kitchen table with three chairs, two chairs for the living room, and a mattress.

The bathtub lacked a shower so I often went downstairs to wash my hair in the large kitchen sink. At one point, when I was in the living room, I thought I saw a rat's head peeking out from behind the stove. Thereafter, I was scared every time I washed my hair downstairs. I imagined the rat lunging at my ankles while my head was underneath the faucet. The landlord set traps.

The kitchen floor tiles seemed to have absorbed years of dirt. The living room radiator sported three colors: one half was light green, one quarter silver, the other quarter brown. The yellow walls were fine. However, the dining area's lower wall had ugly brown paneling. Above it, the wallpaper featured flowers and paisley designs in orange, gold, brown, black, and white.

I wouldn't say the walls were thin, but my astute hearing made them seem so. Thirty-five years ago I could hear a neighbor scrambling eggs in her kitchen. A recent hearing test revealed my hearing is as sharp as a twenty-year-old's. It's a blessing and a curse.

The neighbors, a young couple, were a problem. I was a reluctant witness as their relationship crashed its way to an end. Their fighting was terrible. I shivered. I should have bought ear plugs but didn't know enough to do so. I shared my concern with friends, who might have thought I was exaggerating, which Cubans have a tendency to do. The reality was verified when they visited and heard the fighting.

Relationships were difficult to navigate and manage. I had failed at a few by then. No permanent commitments had resulted with any of the men I dated, though some were interested in pursuing one. Years later, I understood I was too young. Domestic life was hard work. I feared I couldn't cope with a professional life and my own family.

And so my days began to get their rhythm. Weekdays, from Laurel Avenue I walked four blocks to catch a bus on Marshall Avenue. I switched to another bus downtown, and then got off near the high school. I walked another two blocks. On the sidewalks, I passed groups of students gathered before the school day began. Sometimes they smoked cigarettes or passed a joint.

"Good morning, Ms. Veiga," one who knew me might offer.

I'd return the greeting and keep walking. It wasn't my job to report any one. I didn't hear anything about that during my initial interview at the school or at any other time.

My high school days were so different.

The teachers and administrators at Our Lady of Lourdes Academy in South Miami made it clear that we girls represented the school, even on weekends and after school hours. Therefore, if we were wearing a uniform and behaving in ways that were not reflective of its Christian values, we were liable. Discipline was certain. Penalties included suspension or expulsion. The extent of the school's jurisdiction seemed unfair.

An important part of my education was obtained in the classrooms of Humboldt Senior High School. In addition to those of European descent, the student population was Native American, Mexican American, Puerto Rican, Vietnamese, and African American. I had never worked with such a diverse group. There was so much to learn from them. This fact held great appeal.

Many of Humboldt's bright students, I hoped, would go to college.

In particular, there was a young man who read and wrote voraciously. However, he also enjoyed using street drugs. One day, when classes were changing, I saw him in the stairwell. His face showed signs of a mind that was floating in another dimension. He was high.

"What's going on?" I asked.

"Angel dust," he said.

I thought he was going to tip sideways and fall, but no: he kept on standing in front of me. Then he turned and started on the next flight of stairs.

I could see angel dust was a powerful drug. I didn't report him. I didn't know what to do so I kept quiet. In that way, I reasoned, the lines of communication would remain open. I might be more helpful that way. In my journal I recorded my concern, wondering if the young man would someday believe in God.

"Dear God, please believe in him," I wrote.

After my mother's death I stopped going to Mass. While I remained angry with God for taking my mother, I still prayed.

Two young, bright women, one was Native American, showed an interest in literature. I encouraged them. When I asked about their plans after high school, one reported she was pregnant. The other said she was moving in with her boyfriend.

I wanted to grab a megaphone and scream "NO" from the school's rooftop.

I anguished over their choices. I discussed it with Mr. Michael Tweeton, the teacher with whom I worked the majority of the time. He understood. Having spent most of his professional life in the classroom, he knew there were limits to a teacher's influence. High school graduates were young adults, after all. They would have to make their own way, bumping their heads against brick walls while learning life lessons. The description of the process resembled my own.

This philosophy was difficult for me to accept. Americans, it seemed to me, pretty much left you alone, unless you asked for help. They minded their own business. At this time I didn't know many other hyphenated Americans, who might behave differently. I did know, however, that Cubans—including strangers met on the bus—freely piled on advice and shared opinions about what a person should do without being asked.

Recently, a man who was putting a new roof on Glenna's house in Jacksonville, Florida, said he'd worked in Miami for a while. He hired Cuban workers as foremen and managers, he said, because they were skilled in telling others what to do.

Furthermore, I was not aware of how higher education was changing to accommodate nontraditional students. Those two young women may not have been college-bound the following September. However, they might have decided to sign up for classes a year or two later. No coaxing on my part would make them adopt my path. My desire was for them to use their talents, and they were talented enough to excel in college.

Because of my Spanish language skills, I was assigned a young Puerto Rican man who had recently arrived in the Twin Cities via New York City. At nineteen, he was a little old for high school, sort of borderline, actually. He needed to learn English so he enrolled in the bilingual education program, which was in its early years.

At one point, with the support of a Spanish teacher, I advocated for school memos to be translated into Spanish. Parental involvement was crucial to students' education and well-being. I was committed to easing the way a little for Spanish-speaking immigrants. In time, I knew, the parents would learn English.

But they couldn't afford to be in a fog until then. It didn't seem fair when we had the ability to translate for them. At a teacher's meeting, I believe it was the art teacher who recalled that Norwegian was a second language once in Minnesota. It was used in public and taught in the schools. I was grateful for her support.

The office staff, however, was troubled. A secretary complained, "I can't type in Spanish!" Eventually, a memo in Spanish was typed and distributed. I wondered about the resistance.

Often, I spoke Spanish with the Mexican American students, though not all spoke it. Their families had settled years before. At Humboldt Senior High I learned a little more about their community.

Guadalupe Alternative Programs, named after the beloved Virgin of Guadalupe, was located in the neighborhood. It was referred to as the Guadalupe Center, founded by Sister M. Giovanni in 1967. She was one of the School Sisters of Notre Dame. She worked to address the scholastic needs of high-school dropouts. The center continues to provide alternative educational programs.

On January 14, 1980, a journal entry documents my first experience standing in front of a class to teach a little of what I knew about poetry. I explained to the class that in poetry, rural landscapes or "the country" represents a peaceful, simple life. The countryside represented innocence. In contrast, a city landscape represented complications and loss of innocence, a corrosive experience.

A student named David was in the classroom. He had spent some time doing farm work. He listened.

He raised his hand. I called on him.

"Hard work in the country," he said. "Who are you trying to kid?"

When winter came, an English teacher named Mary was kind enough to offer me a ride to work in the morning. I accepted the offer. It was a help, though I still walked six or seven blocks in the dark to her house. I dressed warmly. I wore a blue down jacket, which Mimi's brother Jim had sewn from a kit. Her sister Robbie had made me down mittens. I wore leather tie-up boots lined with wool.

Mary was attractive, articulate, and competent. Her winter wardrobe was beautiful and I admired the quality of her sweaters and skirts. She introduced me to the local poet and artist Alvaro Cardona-Hine, who came from Costa Rica to the United States when he was twelve years old.

In many ways, I was happy. In a journal entry dated February 18, 1980, I wrote, "I live alone and pay my bills. But sometimes, like today, when the wind is warm although there is snow, I want to lift my hand and wave at the sun and sit on a bus bench and soak up the sun with my face like I used to do on the beach so my face would be rosy."

On weekends, I packed two pillowcases with dirty clothes and sheets and walked to the laundromat on Marshall Avenue. A friend who worked at a food co-op let me shop there. He passed on a member discount to help me pay for groceries. I recall two or three visits to see a doctor. One was an annual gynecological examination at a clinic with sliding fees. The other was an annual physical at a doctor's office on the West Side. At that doctor's office, I suspect, I caught the Russian flu.

The symptoms were evident: I was coughing and terribly sick with a high fever. I had no one to drive me to a doctor for a diagnosis and prescription.

Fortunately, a Persian friend called and heard my voice. Immediately, without my asking, he came to the duplex. He found vegetables and chicken and rice and made a delicious soup. He spent the night on the floor in the next room. In the morning, he drove me to the doctor's office. He drove me home.

I will never forget his selflessness.

With most of my friends dispersed, I developed friendships with young women who were writers working other jobs. Mary "Max" Koller was a poet. I met her while working as an intern at a literary distributorship called Bookslinger. During our free time, we met and read and critiqued one another's poems. We looked at art. We talked and drank wine. Sometimes, I cooked or she cooked. They were simple meals.

One memorable event was when she hung an Andy Warhol print—a portrait of Mick Jagger. She was crazy about it, and rightfully so. I am sure it still hangs in her home and continues to bring joy.

The last time and certainly the first time I played hockey since childhood was at her parents' house. Max was a great hockey player who later joined a women's team. One of Max's younger brothers had made an ice rink in the side yard. I donned skates and went out on the ice. Everyone buzzed around me. I attempted to play and skate and fell forward. The air was knocked out of my lungs. That was the last time I pulled on skates.

Susan Pauley was another new friend. I don't recall the circumstances surrounding our meeting, but it was Susan who was responsible for opening a door of opportunity to the next phase of my life. She was headed to a graduate program, a master of fine arts in creative writing, in Bowling Green, Ohio. She wrote fiction.

Susan lived in Minneapolis with her parents and brother. She had long reddish curly hair and multiple piercings on both ears, uncommon at the time. She wore fun sort of hippie-inspired ethnic clothing. She was confident in ways I was not. She had a clear plan and didn't hesitate to claim and follow it. She liked ethnic diversity, she loved music. She introduced me to fabulous Mexican food in St. Paul.

Halloween is the day before my birthday. The following day I would turn twenty-two and I was sad as I knew I'd be alone. So, in order to celebrate it in some way, I bought a bottle of white wine. Once a week, I bought a $5 bottle. The attendant at the local liquor store made recommendations and shared information about each one.

While I've never been a heavy drinker, that night I must have drunk more than the usual. I lay on the mattress in the dark in my work clothes.

Downstairs, costumed kids pounded on the door. They wanted their treats. I had forgotten to buy Halloween candy. So I stayed quiet in the dark. I was dizzy. What would become of me? I wondered. The kids continued pounding.

A question arose: What am I doing here?

In order to improve my understanding, I pictured myself as a character in a novel and reviewed the circumstances. I'd been taught to do this in the analysis of fiction. What factors contributed to the main character's action or inaction?

Despite the joys of friendship, my community of friends had dispersed like the colored stars of fireworks. After my mother's death, the same dynamic had arisen, like a huge wave. Exile was change. Then, I viewed change as a monster that came to shatter a perfectly good status quo.

The elements contributing to a sense of belonging—place, family, and friends—were subject to the rules of change. The weather, for example, was cold and would get colder. The outdoor natural light would lessen with winter's approach. Furthermore, romantic relationships had failed. Each attempt crashed for its own reason. My family in Miami rarely called, though sometimes I received a letter.

The next step, I concluded, was to establish my own home, alone. I needed more education and training in order to be able to make a middle-class living. I will buy myself a house; I will live in it alone, I thought.

That spring of 1980, as the end of the public school year approached, I remember going to a vegetarian restaurant with Susan and a few others. It was a farewell party for everyone, as friends poised to scatter again. I resolved to return to my father's house in Miami. The intention to save money and apply to graduate school propelled me.

Toward the end of the meal, breathing became difficult. I didn't know what was happening or how to stop it. Susan called it a panic attack. This was the first one. Panic attacks are a physiological symptom of post-traumatic stress disorder. Along with my emotional devastation, the trauma of my mother's death in 1974 left this physiological imprint.

I gave away my heaviest winter clothes. Fariba and her friend Roya were moving into the duplex. The furnishings stayed.

And then, I packed my suitcase and a green trunk. I don't remember the move.

Years passed. I didn't need a mortgage. I needed God and myself. The loved ones who have died are in their eternal home; simultaneously, they are in my heart and imagination.

For now, home is an internal space.

I live where I stand.

EPILOGUE

Wooden kiosks sprinkle the east side of Cojímar Bay on Cuba's north coast near Havana. Beyond them, a tall chain link fence protects the town's fishing cooperative. More than likely, those fishermen continue to supply La Terraza restaurant. It is one of Hemingway's haunts, a tourist destination. Their tables are reserved and they come in busloads.

From Havana, my friend Tina Bucuvalas and I took a $10 taxi ride to the village of Cojímar. We got out of the cab at the small business area, where we poked around for a few minutes, agreeing on its charm.

Then we walked the rim of Cojímar Bay from west to east to the kiosks. For more than fifty years, I waited for the day when I would return to my hometown. Seeing the house was key, yet I dodged it. Tina was encouraging. Finally, I was ready to climb the hill to find the house.

To confirm the road went in the right direction, I decided to ask someone and approached a small group of men talking in front of a kiosk.

"Yes, that road takes you up; it connects with the main street," one man said, pointing with a cigarette in hand.

The dirt road was easy as it cut diagonally across the hill. We walked steadily past houses and buildings and pastures with goats. We paused to admire a newborn goat.

We walked until we reached the sidewalk. It began in the business district and ran to the top of the hill.

A woman wearing a uniform watched us from a chair on her front porch. She didn't need an explanation. We asked if we were on the right path.

"There are some very good houses up there," she said. "They belonged to those who left."

We continued uphill. Soon, we met two women on the sidewalk. One was a health-care worker checking for dengue fever; the other was an architect and history buff. We exchanged greetings and explained our purpose. They offered to take us to the house.

The hill is not steep but rises steadily. It's a climb. A few blocks farther up, we turned east onto a short street. I had heard guards were posted still at the bottom of the street. People couldn't pass beyond that point. No one we knew had been able to see our house. I prepared for the inevitable NO. In fact, it was the only scene I had imagined.

Much to my surprise, guards weren't posted. I would see our house on stilts. I would make it home.

Fidel's house was at the end of the street behind dense vegetation.

"There it is, Tina. Those are the steps and the rock," I said, going forward to the steps. It had been a long climb—I didn't know what else to do.

Someone must have alerted the director and her staff, for soon the front door opened. Our small group was welcomed into my former living room turned classroom. We were in the

Sierra Cojímar Polytechnical School for Construction. We were introduced to a slim man who was its founder.

"Do you want us to move the tables and chairs?" someone asked when I expressed a desire to take a photo.

"No, no, it's fine," I said, then went to the opposite end of the classroom and raised my hands on the wall. "The kitchen was here."

"Yes, yes, it was. We made some changes," he said. "Tell your father the roof has not leaked all these years."

I went onto the balcony adjacent to the classroom, a long one with ironwork. I looked down to the backyard where two small classroom buildings had been erected. The backyard, not the front yard, was the setting of my early memories.

A delicious breeze blew. What a view, I thought, the houses and small buildings descending the slope, the tropical vegetation. Beyond these was the horizon of dark blue sea. No wonder my parents' desire was to be buried on the property.

I would have lived there forever.

I closed my eyes to feel the breeze.

Immense joy and terrible sorrow arrived simultaneously. They consumed me with equal power.

It was a bicultural experience of a different kind.

The loop closed. My original home was standing. It had little to do with solid peace inside myself. More than fifty years of longing for home ended.

We thanked everyone and said our goodbyes. Tina and I walked downhill to La Terraza for a good fish lunch.

St. Augustine is a beautiful coastal town in northeast Florida. Once, the Spanish controlled this territory from colonial Havana. For now, it is the right place to live. My husband and I have done so for a decade.

Sometimes, I suggest moving elsewhere. A Latin American country might be right. Old people receive more consideration there. Maybe we could go to Seattle, his home town. Certainly, there's a lakeside cabin for us somewhere in northern Minnesota. He listens while I dream.

I can live anywhere now. I will be home.

⌈ SOURCES ⌉

page 4   John F. Thomas, "Cuban Refugees in the United States," *The International Migration Review* 1 (1967): 46–57.

page 11   Carl J. Bon Tempo, *Americans at the Gate: The United States and Refugees during the Cold War,* Politics and Society in Twentieth-Century America (Princeton, NJ: Princeton University Press, 2015), 107.

page 15   Maria Cristina Garcia, *Havana, U.S.A.: Cuban Exiles and Cuban Americans in South Florida* (Berkeley: University of California Press, 1996), 22, 37.

page 23   Maria de los Angeles Torres, *In the Land of Mirrors: Cuban Exile Politics in the United States* (Ann Arbor: University of Michigan Press, 1999), 37.

pages 27, 33   Carlos Eire, *Learning to Die in Miami: Confessions of a Refugee Boy* (New York: Free Press, 2010), 30.

page 29   Frederick L. Johnson, *Goodhue County, Minnesota: A Narrative History* (Red Wing, MN: Goodhue County Historical Press, 2000), 48.

pages 43, 58   Donald Senior and John J. Collins, eds., *The Catholic Study Bible*, 2nd ed., New American Bible (New York: Oxford University Press, 2011).

page 73   Costica Bradatan, "The Wisdom of the Exile," *New York Times,* August 16, 2014.

page 99   Samuel Hynes, *The Growing Seasons: An American Boyhood Before the War* (New York: Viking Penguin, 2003), 49.

page 123   Henri J. M. Nouwen, *Reaching Out: The Three Movements of the Spiritual Life* (New York: Doubleday, 1966), 84.

page 155   Mary Morris, *A Mother's Love* (New York: Nan A. Talese, 1994), 114.